Extremophilia

*River Rats, Timber Tramps,
Biker Trash, and Realtors*

EXTREMOPHILIA

by

Fred Haefele

Bangtail
Press

Montana
2011

ISBN-13: 978-0-9828601-3-7

Manufactured in the United States of America

The author and publisher would like to thank the following publications in which versions of these pieces originally appeared, often under different titles: "Demon Beetles of Thunder Drive," *Outside*; "Billionaires without Boundaries," salon.com; "Slime and Transfiguration," *Montana Magazine*; "Redwood Brigade," *New Madrid*; "Auguring the Great Divide," newwest.net; "Lost Tribes of Indian," *American Heritage*; "Under the Rapids," and "Confessions of a Timber Faller," *Big Sky Journal*; "Guggenheim's Art of the Motorcycle," "More than a Hiding Place," and "Fire on the Mountain," *Newsday*; "Rebel with a Pacemaker," *The Missoulian*; "Blackfoot Days," *Headwaters Anthology*; "Heartshot," *Game Journal*.

Cover photo of the author courtesy of the author.

Back cover author photo by
Helena photographer Eliza Wiley.

Published in the United States by

Bangtail Press
P. O. Box 11262
Bozeman, MT 59719
www.bangtailpress.com

For Caroline, always.

Contents

Introduction

At my editor's request, I'll speak briefly to this collection of essays, all written over the last twenty years. They are extremely diverse in subject—from an upscale developer in Montana's Paradise Valley to "Wino Willie" Forkner, founder of the seminal Booze Fighters Motorcycle Club. And they are even more diverse in venue, from America's largest toxic waste site to the Guggenheim Museum in Manhattan. For this reason I felt they'd earned the right to a freshly-minted neologism for a title; Stemming from the term "extremophile" (an organism able to thrive in hostile and unlikely environments), if I've done this right, extremophilia refers to an intemperate love of these admirable creatures who live wherever they damn well want to.

Foreword

by

Steven Rinella

I'll always remember the first time that I hung out with Fred Haefele, even though it wasn't actually the first time that I hung out with him. This bit of confusion has to do with the fact that I was enrolled in Fred's writing class at the University of Montana at the time. We'd been together two days a week for a month or so, in class and sometimes at the bar afterward. But even though I found Fred to be a fine teacher and great drinking partner, I'm reluctant to count those experiences as bona fide instances of "hanging out."

Instead, our first time hanging out occurred somewhere in the middle of the semester, after I got word that Fred happened to own his own tree service. He did the work as a sort of hobby-occupation that allowed him to stretch his legs a bit and earn a little extra dough. This was particularly interesting to me, as I happened to have experience in that line of work and I also happened to be extremely broke. One day after class, I approached Fred and explained that I was handy enough with a chainsaw that I wouldn't cut my hands or feet off while using one. Thankfully, he trusted me.

The next afternoon, Fred picked me up at my house in an orange 1967 Chevy pickup. I'd say that this pick-up was vintage, but that might imply that Fred treated it with vintage-like softness, which he certainly did not. It just happened to be an old truck, piled in the back with brush, two chainsaws, and a climbing harness.

Right away I noticed that Fred is a very slow driver. I think this is because he likes to breathe in the history and vibe of the places that he passes through—as well as to comment on them—and to drive fast would create such a tremendous rush of material that his chest would blow open under the pressure. As we followed a circuitous route through town, he pointed out to me places where he used to live, places where he likes to drink a beer now and then, places where an ancient glacial lakeshore lapped at the surrounding mountainside, a place where Blackfeet warriors ambushed their enemies.

Eventually we ended up toward the eastern edge of downtown, near the Albertsons. We turned left on Van Buren and crossed the railroad tracks and went under I-90 and then started creeping our way up the Rattlesnake Valley. Fred pointed out hillsides where it's possible to see elk grazing in the winter, and driveways where you might see a screenwriter checking his mail in the afternoon. A few twists and turns later and we ended up at the home of his client. A black bear had visited her beloved pear tree, basically raping and pillaging the thing. In its efforts to get at the tree's fruit, the bear had shredded the bark and busted off half the limbs.

Fred walked out to his truck and grabbed a small chainsaw and a pole saw and cleaned up that tree as carefully as a practitioner of bonsai. When he was through, he let me take a couple swipes at it as well. The patient emerged from surgery a tad smaller and still a bit haggard, though perfectly healthy. It would live.

We got back into the truck and inched down the valley and back into town. At an intersection on Orange Street, Fred told me a story that had happened to him there some years back. He'd been away from Montana on one of his wanderings, and when he got back to Missoula he couldn't figure out why exactly he'd come. What was it about this place that kept luring him back? He was thinking about this when he pulled up to the intersection. And here came a woman who was obviously eight or nine months pregnant. She was riding a mountain bike, peddling hard and fast, in a skirt. With a bare midriff. Oh, thought Fred, that's what it is about this place: it's here that pregnant chicks come blasting past on bikes.

When I learned that Fred was going to call his new book *Extremophilia*, I immediately imagined the things that must pass through his brain when he thinks of that word. The pregnant bicyclist was among them. But then it occurred to me that I didn't know what the word actually meant. So I looked it up, and found that it refers to organisms that thrive in "physically or geochemically extreme conditions that are adverse to most life on earth."

I'd say that those are definitely the sorts of conditions that can be found in Montana. And while I've never mentioned this to Fred, I was feeling the pressure of those conditions on the day that we first drove around. I was newly arrived from my home state of Michigan, and I was generally feeling overwhelmed by the place. This was the state I'd dreamed of, the Big Sky. I'd come in order to make new friends, find work, experience true wilderness, become a writer. But in reality I didn't have a single real friend; I didn't have a job; I was intimidated by the magnitude of the wilderness; and I had never actually met a real writer except for the ones I met by signing up for classes. Obtaining the life I wanted here in Montana seemed about as realistic as obtaining it up on the moon.

But driving around with Fred that day began to change some of that. Suddenly I could imagine having a friend; it seemed as though I had found a job; and I had just gone up and trimmed a genuine bear-mauled tree with a real-life writer. Things were looking up in the Big Sky.

A lot of time has passed since then. I lived in Montana for eight or nine years, with various stints in Wyoming, California, Alaska, Rhode Island, and now New York. Fred and I have stayed friends through it all. However, in a weird way, I've come to despise Montana. That's because Montana makes every other state seem like a pretty sucky place. Once you let Montana get into your veins, living anywhere else is tough. Soon you start to wish Montana didn't even exist, because then you'd be a hell of a lot happier wherever you ended up.

Based on your decision to pick up this book, I'm assuming that you can understand where I'm coming from. Whether you're in Miles City or New York City, Kalispell or Cleveland, you probably recognize that there's something in Montana that is hard to pin down but that keeps you wanting more. If I'm right about this—and I think I am—you're going to be glad you own this book. Now, when someone asks you what it is about Montana, you don't have to pray for a pregnant mountain biker to come blasting past. Instead, you can just refer them to your favorite chapter.

....

Confessions of a Faller

There was a time when the logging woods conjured images of something other than cataclysmic clear-cuts, stream pollution, and habitat depletion. The logging woods were a place to prove yourself, a rough and tumble arena where tiny men manipulated huge trees on a slender hinge of wood. A place where if you did everything right, there was a good living to be made. And if you did something wrong, it could cost you your life. Thus the logging woods became a kind of headwaters for a stream of American mythologizing, a place that spawned the likes of Paul Bunyan, who felled a hundred trees with a stroke of his axe, or Ken Kesey's only slightly less hyperbolic Hank Stamper.

Certainly it was this kind of mythos that lured me to the Montana woods. In 1977 I was a New England tree surgeon when a string of hard times finally convinced me to try my luck somewhere far away. By the end of that summer I had immigrated to Boulder, Colorado.

In fair weather I climbed hundred-foot cottonwoods for a local tree service. In winter I worked as a sawyer, cutting ponderosa beetle-kill for the Colorado State Forest Service. It was midwinter in the arid high country around Nederland that I first began to hear stories about the great woods of the northern Rockies. The one that sticks in my mind featured an unusual technique employed by Montana winter loggers: First, they shoveled down through six-foot snowdrifts to make their felling cuts at ground level. Then, the story went, as the tree began to go over and the trunk began to rise, the faller would grab his saw, leap aboard, ride the tree up out of the snow—well, like a giant green bronco. These stories were told by my fellow crew members with perfectly straight faces, and I have no reason, even now, to believe they thought them anything less than the Gospel truth.

I know I bought it. Not the tree-bronc business, perhaps, but the accompanying and very potent notion that wherever you happened to be in the West, the real action was always somewhere else: the next state, the next drainage, the next ridge over.

A year in the east-west Boulder glitz gave these stories time to germinate, and finally the country up range drew me north. North, to where the winters were long and tough. Where the woods were full of grizzlies, the trees thick as culverts. North to Montana, where the real action was.

Thus it was that in 1979 I spent a summer east of Lincoln, felling trees for a gyppo I'll call "Bob." I was raring to go, would have signed on with the devil, but even my Job Service counselor puckered with distaste when he handed me the slip with Bob's number on it.

Bob was a relative newcomer to the logging woods,

yet simply everyone had heard of him. From all accounts he was crooked, rapacious, sleazy. In short, he had all the credentials of a highly successful logging contractor. Gangly, boyish, and sullen-looking, he hailed from Dayton, Ohio, just another guy from back east who'd come to Montana looking for the real action. In that sense, except for the trust fund he'd used to set himself up, he was probably a good deal more like me than I cared to admit.

We worked a hundred-acre sale up Copper Creek, butting the Scapegoat Wilderness to the north. It was a private sale, belonging to an out-of-stater (a term for which I quickly learned the proper disdain). Montana is unique among the timber-producing states in that it has no laws governing forestry practices on private lands, so basically the sale was a kind of free-fire zone for a gyppo like Bob.

It was mostly lodgepole with an occasional pocket of old-growth fir, what we called "pickles." The ground was easy, the lodgepole were about seventy feet tall, averaging twenty inches in diameter. All in all, not a particularly formidable-looking adversary for a man who'd come north to make his mark, wrestling with the giants under the most adverse conditions. But it would do.

In the course of the summer the other fallers came and went, and it was mostly just four of us who worked that sale: the loader man, the cat skinner (the loader man's son), me, and my sawing partner, a beetle-kill colleague I had persuaded to come up from Colorado. I'll call him "Ron."

To save money, Ron and I lived in a wall tent in a meadow close by. We tried, at first, to stay out of Lincoln, which meant no restaurants, bars, or showers. We would stay out as long as we could stand it, generally three days at a stretch.

It was a rainless summer and we were forever covered

with dust, insect bites, nicks, and scratches of various origins. We reeked of saw gas, boot socks, and the sap of conifers. In the belief it would clear a nagging case of dandruff, Ron took to dousing his scalp with vinegar, and at night the tent smelled like a rancid salad.

We ate hundreds of cheese sandwiches. We got so hungry that neither of us had the patience even to open a can. We were paid a flat rate of a dollar a log, and on a good day we'd make a hundred dollars, not bad money at the time. In the interest of simplicity, we grew to think: there's a tree, there's a buck.

As mere beetle-kill cutters, we were dazzled by the production faller's argot. Expressions like "cat face," "spike-top," and "barber-chair" seemed charged, full of magic.

We were dazzled by the equipment. The intermountain log trucks were diesel semis, not the gas-powered straight-jobs we were used to. We noted that the real players wore caulked logging boots, not epicene Vibram lugs. The real players felled with six-cubic-inch saws, not the paltry four-and-half-cubic-inchers we were using. Indeed, the notion of the right saw was something we grew increasingly obsessed with. Though we were aware the real players ran a stable of three or four, at $500 per saw, such an investment seemed well beyond our reach. We preferred instead to think that if we each had the right saw, one that didn't need constant tinkering and maintenance, we would somehow get into the real action.

In the course of that summer, Ron and I went through three chain saws each. More and more the right saw seemed merely to be whatever saw some other faller was using. In a remarkably short-sighted move, at the season's outset I traded my faithful old Stihl for a .357 pistol. I'd succumbed to the idea that, while sawing in the Rockies, I might at anytime have to defend the tent from ravening grizzlies, hell-bent on a cheese sandwich. Ironically, the best use I could have put that pistol to would have been to blow a hole in the mindlessly engineered McCulloch 850 I bought to replace my Stihl.

Except for the ongoing crises with the chain saws, there was little out there to divert us. Nobody tootled on the mouth harp. We never played cards. We were generally too tired. I recall that Ron was reading a novel called *The Thornbirds*, that he seemed always to be reading it. The truth was, once we got past our brief infatuation with the lingo and equipment, the actual logging experience was something of a disappointment. Certainly the work was strenuous, but with the undemanding terrain and the smallish, even-aged lodgepole, it soon grew monotonous, even mechanical: there's a tree, there's a buck.

With the arrival of Friday night, we would wait for Bob to show up with our checks (an arrangement that became more haphazard as the summer progressed), then we'd follow the Blackfoot downstream, ninety miles west in my old Dodge pickup, blowing through the bends, driving like Billy BeDamned to arrive back in Missoula in time for Happy Hour. We'd sit, freshly scrubbed and flummoxed in some sad-looking Front Street bar, Ron feeding the jukebox quarters, while it gradually sank in that most everyone had left town for the weekend, that the real action was somewhere else.

We tried to live what we thought was a logger's life, but our vision lacked verve and imagination. What we settled for resembled, instead, a poorly conceived Bud commercial. We worked hard, we drank hard. Sometimes, after a few beers we would swagger around Front Street looking for trouble. We were stud-horse loggers, fresh from the big woods. But nobody much seemed to give a damn.

As the summer wore on we both grew less talkative,

perhaps even melancholic. The only tape anyone thought to bring was Emmy Lou Harris's "Sorrow in the Wind." In the course of six weeks, Ron claimed to have read *The Thornbirds* four times.

At first such a nuisance, we grew at last to welcome chain saw repairs. They meant we could go back to Missoula midweek, when there was actually someone else around. I recall a Tuesday night that Robert Cray passed through town, playing at the Top Hat. He did a catchy number called "Skin it Back and Hold It," a song that seemed to really speak to Ron and me. I recall the two of us, drenched in sweat, dancing with startling abandon with any woman bold enough to take the floor with us, then finally, in what was surely a dance of madness, with each other.

Lying in that pungent tent in the meadow, I began to have vivid, disturbing dreams. One night I dreamed of topless seraphim brandishing flaming chain saws. I was so moved by it that the next evening we drove back to Missoula and, on the strength of my dream, Ron and I turned in our breakdown-prone domestic models for brand-new Swedish Jonsereds. They were sleek, flame red, gloriously light. They were 5.4 cubes, a player's saw if we ever beheld one.

Or not. We soon discovered that to save weight the handles were made of a plastic so flimsy it split at the slightest tug. By noon the next day, I was eating a cheese sandwich, looking over at Ron and his cracked handle. He was looking back at me and my cracked handle and I knew we were thinking the same thing: our Dream Saws were pieces of crap! We had shelled out a thousand dollars only to fail, once again, to come up with the right saw! Grimly, we jury-rigged the handles with hose clamps and duct tape and kept on working.

A couple of evenings later, Ron and I got up from our evening sandwich and began to saw again, more or less just for the hell of it. We had already made our hundred dollars for the day, but the conversation had grown thin and the Montana twilight lasted well past ten. In a haze of fatigue and indifference, I cut through the boundary of my "strip" (the faller's designated acreage) and followed a thick patch of lodgepole up a hillside that was in all likelihood not even on the Copper Creek sale. I did it because the trees were close together, the cutting easy, the saw running well. Besides, it was common knowledge that Bob stole trees all the time: there's a tree, there's a buck.

It seemed I'd never cut so fast, with such abandon. When I stopped to tank up at the top of the hill, I had a peculiar kind of vision. I looked east, over the current of freshly felled trees in my path, then turned west, to the midsummer sun. It was red, swollen. It seemed to vibrate, wobble on the ridgeline. I felt suddenly light-headed. My skin prickled. I began to laugh and the hackles on my neck rose. I couldn't swear but that my hair didn't stand on end, too.

Years later, while reading *The Odyssey*, I thought I recognized that same sensation: It comes at the point when Penelope's suitors are at her table, stuffing themselves on the last of her stores. It's the night before Odysseus reveals himself, and the gods bring a giddiness down on their company, a strange laughing fit that confuses and terrifies them. They don't know quite what they're laughing at. But they sense, for the first time, that there will be consequences.

The next morning I saw Ron walking off his strip, shock and disbelief on his face. He was packing his brand-new Jonsereds out in pieces. The shroud was fractured, cooling fins snapped off, the bar bent double. He'd been cutting and pinned his saw. In a fit of temper, he'd managed to cut through his hinge. (The "holding wood" between the notch and the back-cut, the hinge is the only means of controlling the tree. Cutting through it is the timber faller's cardinal sin.) The tree had narrowly missed Ron, landed instead on his saw. Instead of feeling relief that he was unhurt, I was furious with him. I was furious with everything. I was tired of our life of melancholy, tired of hearing "Sorrow in the Wind." I was so mad that within half an hour I'd done almost exactly the same thing. I cut through my hinge and lost control. Like Ron I got out of the way, but the tree stove in the muffler of my dream saw, and before noon we were back in the truck, driving ninety miles to the saw shop in disgust and defeat.

The second week in August, Bob tried to move us off Copper Creek onto slimmer pickings and we quit. He looked bemused, then chuckled, wrote us checks and said, "Ain't that the way? You guys about get to know what you're doing then you're off down the road."

This remark wasn't entirely false, though it could be argued that Bob would probably be the last to know if anyone knew what they were doing or not. Still, we drove away in good spirits, feeling well rid of Bob until Ron tallied the checks and figured out Bob had stiffed us for the night we'd cut beyond our strips. We nearly U-turned to give him a good thrashing. We opted instead to slash his tires at a later date and drove 170 miles west to St. Regis, where we signed with an outfit working a sale on Little Joe Mountain.

It was rugged country, skyline, about 7,000 feet elevation, and the ground was too steep for a Cat. I looked at Ron. He looked at me. At last! we thought. The real action! We were so impressed by the vista, the Hahn 99 line skidder, and the boxcar-size de-limbing machine that we didn't immediately notice that the trees weren't all that big here, either. In fact, it took another couple of years for me to understand that the big trees, the ones the players cut, were not just a ridgeline over. Or even in the next state. The big trees, as it turned out, were by then mostly gone.

Our next night in Missoula, Ron hocked his saw, went on a bender, and nearly drank himself insane. For a while I tried to help him, blamed myself for bringing him up to Montana. But in a week's time, we'd gone our separate ways.

With its panorama of root wads, slash piles, and broken tops, the last time I saw the Copper Creek sale, it looked like the site for some tactical weapons test. Virtually every tree we had left standing (anything under fourteen inches in diameter) was broken by the fall of larger trees, scarred, or knocked flat by the Cat. The shorter eight-foot logs we had cut were routinely left to rot because it was too hard to place them on the load. Whatever else you can say about that summer, we certainly did make our mark.

But the trees left their mark, too. After a season in the logging woods with barely a scratch, that autumn I received a cut requiring seventy-five stitches while bucking firewood. Talk about a vista—my leg gaped open like a plate from *Grey's Anatomy*. Before I passed out I could identify the tibia, patella, and the various connective tissues. I was off my feet for a month, and I remember thinking, Good, now I have time to think about all this, maybe even make sense of it. But all I could come up with was that the summer seemed to bring to the surface whatever already haunted us. And when we'd cut everything down, finally, we'd done nothing so much as reveal who we were.

Years later I see that our fits of melancholy might be viewed as a kind of environmental bellwether, that Ron was a man for whom the logging mythology simply no longer worked. Along those lines, this would be a more uplifting story if I were to relate that in time Ron went through detox, got his head on straight, and left the logging woods forever. Instead, Ron went through detox, bought sixteen-inch caulked boots and a stable of saws, and returned to the logging woods with a vengeance. For the next four years he cut timber in Wyoming, Idaho, and Montana. Shortly before he finally quit to become a substance abuse counselor, he related an incident that took place in a roadhouse up the Blackfoot, not far from where we used to saw. It was Thanksgiving Eve, and when his crew stopped for beers on the way home, Ron went in with them to nurse a coke and socialize. The company quickly became rowdy, engaged in an uproarious test of skill; Nothing as obvious as arm wrestling, these jolly timber beasts were taking bets on who could pick up a quarter with his buttocks. Ron finished his story and shook his head. "I don't know, Fred." he said. "Seems like there's a different bunch of guys out there these days."

Summer of 1979 was my last season as a timber faller. That autumn, still dragging a leg, I sat in on a fiction workshop at the University of Montana. I wrote a story about a crazy summer in the logging woods, about disillusionment, about the boundaries of a friendship. It was a flawed story about two flawed men, trying to give their lives shape and meaning by living out a myth.

....

Heart Shot

The first time I walked into a classroom to teach, I was terrified. Autumn of 1989 the Stanford Creative Writing Program had honored me with a lectureship. That was the Good News. The Bad News was I'd never taught a class before in my life, much less at a big-time university where, I was fairly sure, they had little tolerance for jokers, hackers, or poseurs. In a classic case of over-preparation, the night before I'd gone barhopping with a veteran professor so I could pick his brain. Then I'd stayed up till all hours, making reams of bombproof lecture notes and lists of bail-out exercises. As an extra precaution, to bring me luck and stave off incontinence, I carried a talisman in the pocket of my Levi's. It was a .30-06 casing from a hunt my wife and I had been on, two autumns before, when we'd taken a whitetail buck in a clear-cut in northwestern Montana. Somehow I had hung on to it, stored it in a pencil cup that I'd forgotten about till it resurfaced, late that night. I'd never carried a talisman before, so it surprised me when I slipped it in my pocket that first morning.

In a town like Palo Alto, rife with bumper stickers like "Mothers Against Meat" and "Hunt Herbs, Not Animals," you may be asking yourself how it is that a shell casing from a successful deer hunt could possibly be viewed as a good luck charm for an introductory class in creative writing. Good point. To get to the bottom of this phenomenon, we must first take into account the circumstances of the hunt.

November the second, All Soul's Day. Indian summer, and my wife and I were hunting out of her father's cabin in Montana's Swan River valley, north of Seeley Lake. Caroline doesn't shoot, but wanted to come along as a spotter, so we kept together. We'd hunted Friday and Saturday without success, and Sunday evening, on our way back home, we decided to try once more. We hiked the mile of skidder trail, through second-growth larch and doghair lodgepole, and hit the edge of the clear-cut an hour before twilight. We'd been sitting behind a ponderosa blowdown for the better part of an hour when I heard the brush pop over my left shoulder. A moment later, Caroline nudged me. Her lips barely moved when she whispered, "Don't look now, but there's a deer on the tree line."

For the next hundred heartbeats I sat as still as I could till I picked it up out of the corner of my eye. The light was fading and I couldn't tell the sex, but it was solo, browsing along the northern edge of the cut. Whenever its head dropped to graze, I brought my rifle up another notch till I finally got the scope on it, less than a hundred yards away. It had looked smallish, maybe a doe, but in the crosshairs I saw he was a young buck, a 2 x 3, and on the plumpish side. I decided that if he gave me a shot, I would take it.

I rested the Enfield on my knees, tracked him as he moved away, and waited. When he finally turned, I set the crosshairs on his shoulder and squeezed the shot off. He whirled in midair and vanished into the woods. I blinked. Caroline said, "My God, but that thing is loud." Her eyes were wild, round with excitement. I jacked in another round and stood up. It was in that moment, with the roar of the shot fading from a thunderclap to a kind of inner roar, that everything seemed to change, and I was left with an odd kind of foreknowledge, a prescience. It must have been then that I stooped and pocketed the casing.

We found the buck quickly, about thirty yards into the woods. We came up on him from the rear, and although his haunches looked exactly like a small boulder, I knew immediately that it was him. We approached carefully, though I already knew he was dead. The round had taken him just behind the shoulder, and as I tagged him, Caroline was still incredulous. "Are you sure this is ours?" she breathed and I laughed, I don't know why, and said, "My God, Caroline. Who else's would he be?"

She helped me drag him across the pine duff, back into the clear-cut. The light was nearly gone and we had to work fast. I'd only dressed one other animal, so as a precaution I'd brought along a yard sale field guide, Audrey Alley Gorton's *The Venison Book* (1957). Unfortunately, I'd forgotten to bring a flashlight, and one of my fondest memories of that evening is of Caroline in her hunting vest, kneeling in the beargrass with darkness closing in, reading to me by match light: "Take a pinch of skin between thumb and forefinger, pull it away from the body and make a cut..."

I have no idea of the time it took us, but I know we worked swiftly and efficiently together. When the organs came out, they were all intact except for one.

"I can't find the heart," I said.

"The bullet blew it away," Caroline said.

It wasn't a guess, it was a statement of fact. She knew things now, too.

When we finished, it was nightfall. Rather than drag him the mile back, we horsed the buck into a sitting position, draped him over my shoulders, and I carried him downhill, picking my way over the stumps, back to the truck. My legs burned with the effort, but I never doubted we'd make it. We drove an hour and a half back to Missoula, Caroline and I with our dog between us, the buck cooling in the back. We were mostly quiet, but it was still one of the happiest drives I can remember—not because it was a spectacular shot or a Boone and Crockett trophy (though the chops were delicious). It was for something we'd done. Or maybe the way we'd done it. It had something to do with taking the right shot at the right time. Something about how I knew it was the right shot, like almost nothing else I've known. I knew from the way everything seemed to stop and, for a moment, fit together. Things you wouldn't expect to fit together, like triumph and sadness. Like my life and that buck's.

Anyway, in the course of three years of teaching, there was always something I wanted to say to my students about that evening but I wasn't sure exactly what it was, and anyhow, who wants to sound like warmed-over Hemingway? So I never did. But now that the lectureship is over and I'm about to go back to Montana, I guess if I had three years' worth of students all together, sitting with me in a bar, let's say, I would risk telling them something like this: A good line in a good story is like the right shot at the right time. It fills your head with its sound. It echoes, and these echoes connect everything, make things different, but on a level that won't quite let you say how or why. But you know it when you hear it. You know it with more certainty than you ever know anything in your life.

I want to tell them something like that, but the academic community is not one in which a hunting metaphor thrives these days. So while I told my students a lot of things about character, dialogue, point of view, etc., I dummied up about that heart shot, though I carried the brass faithfully for three years. In the academia of the 1990s, a world crammed with issues—sexism, multiculturalism, deconstructionism, and postmodernism—my talisman was a moment in time from years before: the roar of the shot, the look in my wife's eyes. That thing we knew together, whatever it was, with more certainty than we'd ever known anything.

1994

Fire on the Mountain

We've reached the final days of summer. A thick haze shrouds Missoula from fires a hundred miles away. It tints the moon that blooms over the mountain like a neon peach pit, renders it faintly comic. Three days earlier I drove back from Flathead Lake and the moon was a dirty, bloody orange. Dangerous. I made the trip home with a good friend. We had plenty to talk about, but wherever the conversation went, it seemed always to find its way back to that moon.

By September 27, 4,760 fires have been recorded in Western Montana, exceeding the year-end total for all three preceding years. Drive by the laundries and you'll see soot-stained Forest Service sleeping bags piled high at the side doors. The local catering services are doing a land-rush business as a stream of smoke jumpers and Hotshot crews shuttle in and out of town by plane, school bus, helicopter. All day, vintage piston-driven aircraft drone overhead as the slurry bombers land, tank up, fly off on another sortie.

August 5, a fire started on the I-90, just west of town. In minutes, it was headed up Grant Creek towards one of the more recent and affluent housing developments. Less than a mile from the aerial depot, the regional fire fighting center for the intermountain West, the fire was contained in short order with no houses burned, no one hurt. In a season marked by the deaths of twenty-three firefighters, this was a happy ending. Still, Grant Creek brought the serious business of fire home to me in a way the other burns hadn't, and for the first time in years I had a sense that, if you're not out on a fire, you're missing all the action.

Fighting fires is dirty and dangerous. The hours are outrageous, the food is bad. But then there's the money. For these parts at least, the money is terrific. So I called the Lolo National Forest ranger station and put my name on the list.

The last time I volunteered was 1985, when Sentinel, the 5,000-foot mountain abutting the University, caught fire mere blocks from my house. Around 4:00 p.m. I first spotted the smoke. It rose from a gully at the foot of the mountain, twisted like a rattler, then straightened, thickened. Up and down the block everything stopped. Cars pulled over, drivers got out, stood in the street to stare as the scrub brush flared and the whole gully erupted in fire. A column of white smoke massed, rose like cumulus shot with lightning. Soon a line of yellow clad figures appeared, strung out across the ridge as the sky began to fill with aircraft. By five o'clock the fire burned its way a thousand feet higher, then headed east, into Hellgate Canyon. An ex-logger, I put my name on the sawyer's list and was assigned to a fire forty miles east of town.

When I put my name on the list this time, I hung up the phone, poked around in my files, found the Xeroxed daily fire report from that summer nine years ago. I'd forgotten I had it, forgotten the fire I was on was called the "Gilbert Fire," that it was smallish, about four-hundred acres. The sawyers work in two-man teams and, as I read through the list of names, I recall that one of the teams, Fred and Bill Sweet, were father and son. My saw team partner was Collin McLaughlin. He was rail-thin, good with a saw, a tireless, snoose-dipping ex-logger and oil patch worker with thick glasses and the gnarliest arms I've ever seen. Some of the Hotshot crewmen who dug line behind us had names like Pretty on Top, Many Hides, KillsNight. At the end of the report there's a page titled SAFETY. The first item reads: "Watch for burning/falling snags...[they] continue to be a significant safety hazard. Heads up!"

Our first morning on the line, Collin and I were cutting through doghair lodgepole, downhill from the fire. It seemed there were too many of us, that we were bunched up, the Hotshots working too close behind us. I had stopped to gas my saw when a burnt-through snag arced out of the fire and blind-sided a Hotshot kid while he dug line. He did a little cartwheel then went down hard, fifty feet away from me. I heard the Strike Team Leader say, "Is there a man down?" though I was certain that he'd seen it happen too. One by one, the other saws died, the voices seemed to fade, the whole hillside went quiet, and all you could hear was the hiss and pop of the fire. I stood, frozen to the spot. Finally the kid moaned and it seemed to break the spell. I trotted over, light-headed, full of dread, reached him about the time his crewmate did.

The kid's face was ashen. He had a gash along his scalp line and he was lying absolutely still.

"Can you move your legs?" I asked. The kid groaned, turned a shade greyer. His crewmate reached down, took him gently by the chin and the kid screamed high and long. Soon we were circled by the rest of the crew and there was talk of a broken neck. Incredibly, he was beginning to tremble. He was going into shock. Someone covered him with a mylar fire shelter while the Team leader radioed for a chopper, and it struck me how odd it was, watching someone fight for warmth at 112 degrees or whatever it must have been. We stood around, smoked cigarettes, watched him shake as the fire crept down slope toward us. Now and then another snag would crash down, or a log would roll out, tumble past us so that finally, by the time the helicopter arrived, we were all about ready to jump out of our boots.

The paramedics bounded up slope in their Reeboks and flight suits, stabbed the kid with an IV, cinched him into a cervical collar, strapped him on a litter. I watched as they loaded him on the JetRanger, watched it rise in a cloud of prop-wash, and Collin and I exchanged looks as if to say, "Wow, we've been sawing an hour and they're already packing 'em out. If it's going to be like this, should we stick around?"

That night at Fire Camp Bonita, Collin and I stomped the weeds down by my pickup, staked out our bivouac. New crews were arriving and bed-down space was at a premium. I tried to doze off while a cloud of meat smoke drifted by from the cook tent broilers. The camp was lit up like a car lot, lights strung tree to tree, and a gas-powered generator pounded away. I thrashed around most of the night, realized that whatever was or wasn't going on all around me, I probably wouldn't have slept anyway.

The next day we punched it through. Collin and I worked with a single spotter, cut a half-mile of line up the steep terrain of the northwest side, all the way to the landing zone, "Helispot 1." We stayed about five minutes ahead of a BIA crew as the fire closed in from below, and we were never more than a couple hundred feet from the hot stink of its breath. Our saws vaporlocked from boiling gasoline. Our canteens were long spent and my hands cramped from dehydration. At some point I realized if the wind picked up and the fire bored in, our escape route was now uphill, to the landing zone which we now took for granted was close enough to make a run for.

By five o'clock I could see the Day-Glo hardhats of the BIAs against a scrim of flames as they cleared the line Collin and I cut, scraped the mountainside back to rock, working from their hands and knees in the steeper sections. We'd been on the mountain ten hours and, in a haze of fatigue, I forgot about the escape route, forgot about everything. I felt a peculiar kind of weightlessness and, at one point, as we scrambled upwards, it seemed we rode the blasts of heat like hawks on a thermal.

Helispot 1 was a Day-Glo windsock in a cairn. We topped out, discovered a cache of five gallon clear plastic water jugs, piled up like blocks of ice. We'd worked well, sawed like pros, so Collin took one, I took one and we sat down and drank ourselves sick while the world below us—the trees, the rock, even the sky—burned like a pyre.

That night fresh crews arrived in their clean yellow fire shirts, hollering and sailing frisbees past the outhouses till midnight. One crew played a game called "NumbSkull" that seemed to involve a golf ball and six players in hard hats.

I stripped off my socks to examine my feet and the sight of them startled me. Someone had pulled a switch on me—these looked like the feet of an old man. They were dead white, veiny, raw with blisters, cut up badly by a pair of boots I'd had for years. I'd never worn them sixteen hours at a stretch though, and my feet were swollen from the heat, rendering the boots a size too small.

The next morning in the breakfast line, Collin stood next to me, cheerful, tireless. As we moved along, he speared a tepid flapjack, let it hang in the breeze, said, "A cold hotcake. It's so hard to take." At the time, I thought that was the saddest, truest thing I'd ever heard.

Overnight there'd been desertions in the ranks of the sawyers, and the next morning they split up Collin and me, sent me off on mop-up where, for twelve hours, I trudged up and down a very steep fireline, a human yo-yo, felling widow makers and flaming snags while the crews took it easy, swatted hotspots, picked berries.

The next morning I reevaluated things. The fire was contained, I'd made eight hundred dollars. My feet were too sore to get my boots on anyway and that seemed to settle it.

I drove home barefoot, arrived before seven, threw my boots in the trash. I wasn't sure what day it was. To the east, Mount Sentinel was carbon scarred, still smoldering in places. But in the stillness, my backyard was so green and sweet-smelling it was like a miracle. The heads of lettuce, rows of dill weed shone with dew. The zinnias and cosmos glowed in the early light and the house looked still and peaceful, as if it were under a spell. I felt I'd been gone a very long time, that somehow, up there at Helispot 1, I'd lost a whole season.

"Did you put the fire out?" my wife, Caroline, asked me.

"Not exactly," I told her. "But almost."

"How come you're back already?"

I didn't know where to begin, and shrugged. "I got old," I told her. It was supposed to be a joke.

Now we're three weeks past the Perseids meteor shower and the county fair has come and gone. But even with the nights beginning to cool, August flies grimly on with its heat, its furious winds, and dry lightning. Little Wolf. FreezeOut. The Yaak Complex. Starvation Creek. The burns are sprayed about the fire map like birdshot. The forests have a lower moisture content than kiln-dried lumber, so that this summer compares to the summer of 1910, when the entire state of Idaho nearly burned down.

In town life goes on but there is an edge. It's true these are the Dog Days, that annual time of psychic perigee. Yet this is somehow different: An easy-going friend was nearly in a fist fight when he double-parked to pick up his wife and new baby. My wife got into a shouting match in our neighborhood park. Another friend discontinued his evening run along the river. "Too weird out there," he said. In this normally laid-back mountain town, there is a marked aggressiveness in traffic, a surliness on the sidewalks. A local term for this behavior is "owly," and "owliness" is widespread.

We log in the "incidents," tally them in with the scorched raspberries, the desiccated ferns, the patch of sun-scald on the front lawn that won't water away. We have grown to understand that there are the Dog Days, certainly. And then there is Fire Season.

A summer like this is a kind of revelation. When we witness for prolonged periods the combustion of the world around us—when we see it, feel it, breath it—it's bound to cause alarm. It seems it must somehow change everything. It's not just a slow time of the year, it's a summer gone malignant, a most powerful reminder of just how short a time we have.

As hot as the fires burned, I didn't hear from the Forest Service until the Ward Mountain Fire broke out over the weekend. They called me Monday morning, looking for sawyers, but by this time, it was too late in the year and I had other commitments to honor. Still, it took me a full hour of waffling before I finally called her back, told her I just couldn't make this one.

As I recount all this, I think of my remark, nine years ago: "I got old." It was supposed to be a joke because I thought of myself as "only" forty-one. But now I realize in a way, it was true. That up on Helispot 1, I had some prescience that it might be my last summer for such an adventure, and this has proved to be true. To go out and fight a forest fire is, in a way, the ultimate gesture of defiance. It is an attempt to restore our notion of Order to phenomena we generally concede to be well beyond our control. Like, for example, the passage of time. Fire fighting is probably the work of a young person, who doesn't yet know there is a limit to the summers left to burn.

1992

Blackfoot Days

You drive through Milltown and past Harold's Club, roll on past Stimson Lumber with its pitiful-looking decks of pecker-pole pine, past the FWP game check turnout, past the pair of rough-looking hunters' cabins, their deer gambrels swinging empty beneath a cloudless summer sky, and you're into that first big sweeper that winds left along the river. You sweep left, sweep right again, follow the river till you get to mile five. A hundred yards past the mile marker and just over the bridge, by the splintered-up fruit stand and trodden-down fencing, you are confronted with a series of admonishments: NO PARKING! NO TRESPASSING! NO PUBLIC ACCESS! And then, as a kind of afterthought: SWIMSUITS ONLY! There is something about this place—its odd combination of warning and accommodation—that will keep you coming back again and again.

Just over the fence, the field gives way to bunchgrass, the bunchgrass gives way to creek willow, then the bank slides away to a thin crescent of beach, scattered with old fire rings. The beach gives way to a shelf of cobbles that slopes off into the river. And over on the far side, banked by steep, larch-studded talus, there is a swimming hole so deep it goes right to the center of the earth.

One blistering July afternoon a long time ago, when I was still new to this place, I asked the pretty red-headed waitress who served lunch at The Shack to join me for a swim and she did. To make things more interesting, I brought along a bottle of pretty good tequila. To be on the safe side, Annie brought along a couple of her friends.

What was it about that day? Was it Annie, her body a startling white in the frosted green water? Was it the way the river rushed over and around and through us, so fast and cold and powerful?

Back on shore we rubbed ourselves down with towels, then took turns on the tequila bottle as the cars whizzed past, clicking and thumping on the bridge deck fifty feet away. Annie's two friends (they were Germans) laughed at my rendering of Goethe's "Ehrlkonig," a creepy old poem about children, woods spirits, and death. It is the only German I know, and for reasons I cannot now appreciate, I felt called upon then to recite it:

Wer reidet so spat, durch Nacht und wind?
Es ist der Vater mit seinem kind.

"Har, har, har," one of the Germans said after the first verse. He was gasping, weeping with mirth. "You will stop this now, yes? Please?" And I did, eventually, but not until I ran out of verses.

The heat of summer conjoined with melted snowpack;

the scent of willow mixed with the smell of sun-warmed skin. I balanced carefully on the fat, smooth cobbles underfoot, leaned forward, and kissed Annie on the lips, right there in front of everyone: her German friends, some high-flying hawks, and a perfectly dignified-looking prairie dog. Then something happened and the afternoon grew huge, round, and silent.

We returned to town that evening, Annie and I and her two friends. We made our goodnights, got caught up in our respective lives, and never spent another hour together.

Sometime later, I mentioned the swimming hole up the Blackfoot to my friend, Gary. Gary worked for the sheriff's department and he was incredulous.

"You swim in the Blackfoot? Jesus, that's the most treacherous river in the state! There's currents in that river, nobody knows where they go. They'll get you down and hold you under. There's cars and bodies all up and down that river and dozens of guys we've never ever found. You swim in the Blackfoot? Man, you are out of your freaking mind."

Well sure, I thought. It probably is a dangerous spot, but lots of people swim there. That's probably what's so fun about it. But I ended up thinking about that day again and again, about the odd confluence of laughing Germans, elf kings, and a tequila-laced summer day. About Annie's strong white body, the greenness of the water, the power of the current. About that single kiss that seemed to stop everything before our lives, Annie's and mine, carried us away downstream.

1996

More than a Hiding Place

Two weeks ago, my oldest daughter flew into Missoula from DC, and when I picked her up, I said, "Well Kirsten, what would you like to do now that you're here? We could go check out the Kaczynski arraignment in Helena or we could drive over to Jordan and see how the Freemen standoff is going. I mean, it's your vacation and it's up to you..."

It was a joke of course, but like many of my friends, at first I took a kind of perverse pride in Montana's unique brand of celebrity. Certainly not because I espouse the causes of Uzi-slinging racists or sociopathic Luddites. But just because, living in a state with barely 800,000 people, how often do you get to hear the CNN anchor say, "Elsewhere in Montana today..."?

So for a while the gags were coming fast and furious: "Montana—where you're wanted!" or, "Montana: the

Last Best Place...to Hide!"

Significantly, none of these seem particularly funny now. Things turned sour in a hurry, and helping us toward that end were the hordes of journalists that converged on this state like a hatch of black flies and began immediately to draw a stunningly perspicacious series of conclusions:

—That the natural respect country people have for one another's privacy somehow equates to a kind of complicity. (One columnist from Ohio suggested we didn't watch our neighbors closely enough!)

—That the unrelated incidents at Jordan and Lincoln prove beyond a doubt that Montana is a kind of Destination Resort for every whacko, flip-top, and wind chime who ever had an axe to grind.

—That the Jordan standoff and the Kaczynski arrest are very likely a product of the fact that Montana, in 1997, had no legal speed limit....

A good friend drove past Kaczynski's cabin two weeks ago, when the story was still breaking. He said there was a small army of journalists in the yard, brandishing their boom mikes like medieval halberds, grimly laying siege to the place. Posted at the door was a single FBI agent, who would only let them inside two at a time. There was much jostling for position, and at one point the journalists were actually trying to out-credential each other in hopes of gaining preference. "Listen, pal," said one. "I should get in next. I've been to Rwanda!"

"Yeah?" said another. "Well I was in Rwanda and Oklahoma City!"

As if on cue, a rental Taurus suddenly roared into view, bore down on the cabin, hit the brakes hard, and slid to a stop in the gravel. The doors flew open and two journalists bailed out, breathless.

My friend said, "Take it easy, you guys. I mean, you almost hit me."

The driver replied, "Hey. We're on deadline, pal..."

Last weekend, my wife and I loaded our dog and our new baby into the family wagon and drove eighty miles east to have a look at whatever there was left to see in Lincoln.

It's hard to overstate just how small a town it is. Situated on the west slope of the Rockies, roughly halfway between Missoula and Great Falls, for years Lincoln's claim to fame was the coldest recorded temperature (minus 75 degrees) in the lower forty-eight. Before the arrival of the Hi-Country Jerky works, the main industries were outfitting and logging. Along those lines, it's worth mentioning that in 1979 I spent my first summer in Montana working in these same woods. It's also worth mentioning that, at that particular time in my life, I was something of a fugitive, too. A fugitive from an imploding marriage, from a career gone badly awry. To minimize expenses, my sawing partner and I decided to rough it, and throughout the work week we lived in a wall tent on-site. After a couple days cutting timber we would come into town for a beer—wild-haired, covered with dust and pitch. In the end, I suspect, we didn't look all that different from Kaczynski. Nobody ever bothered us, either. To that small town's credit, nobody even batted an eye.

My wife and I stopped at Lambkin's restaurant in the center of town to get a bite to eat. Aside from some graffiti in the men's room that played off the term "pipe bomb," things looked pretty much the same as they had seventeen years ago. It was peaceful and convivial in Lambkin's, and my wife nursed the baby while we ate. I asked the waitress if it was still pretty crazy in town and she nodded emphatically: "Oh yes. We got the boys and girls Class B basketball tournament going on at the same time..."

A heavyset ranch woman in shorts and Reeboks sat across the aisle from us, admired the baby, and we began to talk. The way people do in small towns. At the mention of Kaczynski, she heaved a sigh and scowled. She told us she got so tired of the out-of-towner's disappointment that she didn't know him that she began to tell everyone that she did. "I'd tell them, 'Oh hell yes, I used to shoot pool with Ted all the time.'" She shook her head. "People are so gullible. I mean, I didn't know Ted but sure, I knew who he was all right. He was just another crazy old guy, riding around on a bike..."

In a box by the register was a stack of freshly minted souvenir T-shirts featuring a tiny silk screen of Kaczynski's cabin with a legend that seemed the soul of discretion: MOUNTAIN HIDEOUT OF THE SUSPECTED UNABOMBER.

Nobody seemed to be buying them.

A month after the arrest, the citizens of Lincoln seem to have had quite enough of the press and Ted Kaczynski. Stemple Peak Road, the site of Ted's cabin, is a right turn at the Conoco station in the center of town. I stopped there for gas, walked in to settle up, and grinned at the woman behind the counter. "So," I said. "Where is it?"

She took my money and without so much as a glance up, pointed down the road.

In the time-honored tradition of ghouls and rubber-neckers the world over, I drove my family three miles down Stemple Peak Road in search of Kaczynski's cabin. It was a brilliant spring afternoon. Ranch families were out burning slash piles and the smoke stung our eyes as we drove along, searching for that now famous mailbox.

But the mailbox was gone, uprooted for some crime lab. Or to vex the curious, such as ourselves. All there was to see was a Jeep Cherokee parked across the Kaczynski drive. Inside was a bored-looking female FBI agent in a smart flannel shirt and high-top lace-up boots that looked to be the J. Peterman Amelia Earhart model. I got out to ask how far up the drive we could go, and she told me we'd already gone that far. I can't say I was terribly disappointed but I lingered a moment, tried to make small talk. Like you might do with a neighbor. Like we'd just done in the restaurant in Lincoln. But the agent wasn't from Lincoln. Not with boots like that she wasn't. What's more, she wasn't interested in the baby or in the fact I'd driven all the way out there with my family. In fact, she gave the impression she'd seen my kind before. She'd seen me through the eyes of CNN, 20/20, Dateline, and the like. She'd seen that I was another yahoo from the sticks who bore a little closer watching....

1996

After the Flood

Fifteen thousand years ago, my study here on the Missoula Valley floor was seriously underwater. The peaks surrounding me—today the launch pads for hang gliders—were a string of islands, an archipelago in Glacial Lake Missoula. Two hundred miles downstream in Idaho, the river we now call the Clark Fork was dammed by glaciers, and when it swelled to about the size of Lake Ontario, the ice dam ruptured, releasing "the largest flood of known geologic record" (*Roadside Geology of Montana*, Alt/Hyndman). A two-thousand-foot wall of water ripped west all the way to the Columbia River, flinging boulders around like ball bearings, shearing away hillsides like a hydro-sluice, blasting millions of acres of silt hundreds of miles downstream. In the waning centuries of ice age, until the climate began to warm, the dam reformed, the lake bed refilled, and it happened all over again. This valley filled and emptied a total of thirty-six times, and with a dusting of snow, striations of old shoreline pop out on the west face of Mount Sentinel like the whorls on a topo map.

It was as if there was something here that needed purging. Writer John Hutchens describes growing up in Missoula with "the feeling of big events, in the past or to come. Nature, huge and sometimes ominous, was just outside the door." Perhaps it gave the Salish a similar feeling, as they called this place In My Su Let Ka, "by the chilling waters of awe." In any case, I believe the relentless hydrodynamics that shaped this place—the scores of buildings up and burstings forth—have long been part of the collective unconscious of its inhabitants. That even today, the dream of flood trickles into our lives, dreams, and literature.

At the end of the twentieth century, the Missoulians who are happiest here, I venture, are the people who live to be outdoors. If all the Subarus with their ski racks and all the pickups with the deer rifles in their windows fail to convince you of this, then check out some of the vanity plates, with their cryptic allusions to the licensee's particular enthusiasm: ELKSKR, HOOKNEM, SNOJONZ, O2BHIKIN.

With the Rattlesnake Wilderness just ten minutes north of town, there are hundreds of miles of hiking and biking trails available at the drop of a suggestion. Fishermen from around the world make the pilgrimage to Rock Creek, just half an hour east, and the great rivers that course through town are irresistible to most boatmen, starting with the spring whitewater season and on into the summer, when overnight canoe trips are for many an annual excursion. In autumn, hunting season opens the door to a more serious kind of outdoor experience, and the question around town becomes, "Did you get your elk yet?" With a quarter million acres of roadless area to pack into, the Bob Marshall Wilderness, only ninety minutes away, is a Mecca for hunters, horsemen, and outdoorsmen of every stripe.

Must a Missoulian recreate constantly to make it all seem worthwhile? Well, no. My family and I ski sometimes, take day hikes now and then, and canoe when we can. But I can't tell you what it does for the spirit just to know that it's all right there....

In 1864 Missoula was established at the confluence of three rivers: the Clark Fork, the Bitterroot, and the Blackfoot. A sawmill was built along the Clark Fork's north bank and soon the little town was on its way. The plentiful timber and the unceasing demand for it by the railroad and mining industries eventually made Missoula a thriving lumber town.

By the end of the century the dirt streets had been paved and buildings like the six-story Montana Block and the Palace Hotel, which still provide a kind of high-water mark for Missoula's economic prospects, were erected. Electric trolleys ran the north/south length of Higgins Avenue, and when the cars were routinely vandalized, it became clear that Missoula had entered the twentieth century. As if to underscore this, Fort Missoula, the old frontier garrison west of town, mustered a unit unlike any other before it. Comprised entirely of black men, the 25th Infantry Bicycle Corps rode all the way to St. Louis at the turn of the century before they finally shipped out for the Spanish American War.

Meanwhile, up the Bitterroot Valley, an apple called the Macintosh Premium was growing fat and sassy, and hundreds of city weary Eden-seekers, anxious to start life over, moved west to buy orchards. One of these families was my wife's great-grandfather, who moved here when his infant son suffered from ill health in Chicago. Of all things, John Patterson moved his family to Missoula for the air, a challenging concept, I'm sure, for any of today's residents. But in a matter of months, Patterson believed his future was so rosy with apples that he could barely restrain himself, and he wrote home to tell his family: "I'll make enough money here in a few years so both of you and Kate will have more than they no [sic] how to spend. This is the place for the whole crowd to come and cut out all worrying..."

By comparison to Montana's famed reputation as Big Sky Country, Missoula feels closed in. The town sits in a kind of three-sided box, the eastern edge abutting a pair of grassy, spud-like mountains, Mount Sentinel and Mount Jumbo (named after Barnum and Bailey's famous elephant). In summer the sun doesn't clear the ridgeline until hours past daybreak. The narrow drainage to the northeast halts at the mountainous Rattlesnake Wilderness, and the rugged, hundred-mile span of the Bitterroot range stretches off to the south. The only real vista is to the west, where the valley broadens into riparian prairie as far as the eye can see.

Through most of the summer, the rivers run green and powerful and Missoula looks lush, prosperous. The maple-lined streets pool with shade, and by evening the day's heat dissipates quickly in the mountain twilight. In the winter, with its valley inversions and monochrome textures, the town looks harsh, like some battered black-and-white photograph, and the snow highlights things other than ancient shoreline. Like the way the mountainsides are pocked and scarred with patch cuts, burns, and logging roads. Like the numerous abandoned lumber mills that all point to the decline of the once thriving timber industry.

And a few miles east of town, near the confluence of the Clark Fork and the Blackfoot, there is an ominous concentration of metals. Washed a hundred miles downstream from Butte's notorious Silver Bow Creek, these tailings are further evidence, as if any were needed, of the party-on environmental insouciance that was for so long the signature of the western extractive industries. Indeed, this site boasts such a smorgasbord of heavy metals—arsenic, copper, zinc, and cadmium—that if water could somehow be smelted (a process actually under investigation in Butte), it might be worth millions.

But Missoula is unique for another kind of confluence. It's a place where Coastal Cosmopolitan meets Western Chic, where techno-recies meet intermountain shit-kickers, where Cowboy Schmaltz meets Seattle Grunge. With a population of around 75,000, depending on who's doing the counting, it's the hometown of mezzo-soprano Judith Blegan, pioneer suffragist Jeannette Rankin, Olympic gold medalist Erik Bergoust, and a rare species of bird called the indigo bunting. It's been home to movie star Andie MacDowell and rocker Huey Lewis, and in a state where there is perennial legislation for the reinstigation of spanking in public schools, Missoula is a bastion of liberals. Liberals, but not bleeding hearts. The town supports a ninety-piece symphony orchestra and averages three firearms per household. It hosts an international choral festival, a wildlife film festival, one of the better attended pow-wows in the Northwest, and a Gay Pride Day. It is the home of the first wooden carousel built since the Great Depression. It is headquarters for the largest touring children's theater company in the country, the home of orchard-burglarizing bears, bad-apple mountain lions, and a resident street person in full leprechaun attire who claims to be Jewish. It has the country's first Smokejumper Training Center, a fledgling semipro baseball team, and its own French Consul Honoraire. Perhaps this is why every few years a team of French journalists shows up to rediscover the place. The July 1995 *Le Pointe* magazine puts it this way: "A coup d'état has taken place in the American literary world without anyone noticing. Forget New York, Los Angeles, or Chicago, the new literary capital of the United States is called henceforth Missoula...(which) counts more writers per square foot than any other town on the North American continent, Greenwich Village included."

Ever since U of M's Professor H. G. Merriam founded the literary magazine *Frontier* in the 1930s, the place has had a peculiar attraction to writers, who arrive here regularly on some kind of twentieth-century version of a vision quest. Sometimes they come for a conference, sometimes for a semester at the University. Sometimes they come to stay, and sometimes, or so it seems, they come just to get their photographs taken with their pointy-toed boots propped on some obliging Montana desk top. But from 1964 to 1982, they gathered here to study with the seminal teacher/poet Richard Hugo, or with prose writer William Kittredge, or because it was so beautiful and so inexpensive to live. But things, of course, have changed. Still beautiful? Yes. Inexpensive? Not by a long shot.

Still the writers come. According to James Crumley (*The Last Good Kiss*, *Border Snakes*, etc.) the reason goes something like this: "Missoula used to be at the bottom of a lake. Writers like damp, sticky places." Whether you buy into any of this or not, it's true there are a couple of famous books that are simply inseparable from this town. Most everyone knows Missoula is *The Last Best*

Place (edited by Annick Smith and Bill Kittredge) where *A River Runs Through It* (by Norman McLean). And it's certainly true the traffic in literati exceeds that of cities many times its size. Some of the most famous American writers of the late twentieth century—Raymond Carver and Richard Ford, James Lee Burke, Ian Frazier, James Welch, and Annie Dillard—have come to Missoula to teach or to live, or just to sport and socialize, to exchange stories of transcendental irony and unsurpassed hilarity in one of this town's many cave-like, majestically slow-moving western barrooms.

Maybe this raconteur-fest really began when Mark Twain passed through in 1895 and found himself outmatched by the men of Colonel Burke's Fort Missoula post, who proved to be such relentless and voluble storytellers that a repeatedly-interrupted Twain finally became distraught. "I beg you," he exclaimed. "Just give me one chance!" Significantly, the only existing photo of this fabled event features the back of Twain's head.

This would not be a piece about Missoula if I neglected the bar scene, which in no small way has long been a kind of signature of this place. Many of Missoula's bars, from the Oxford to the EastGate Lounge, have appeared in fictional guise in various works of literature. Surprisingly for such a small town, most of Missoula's bars are models of big-city tolerance and egalitarianism, with the professor and the poet, the smokejumper, the freight hopper, and the cross dresser amiably bellying up together for happy hour; and at bars like the Missoula Club, Charlie B's, and the Union Hall there is generally a remarkable conviviality that some might view as the town at its best. Take, for example, the former Front Street biker bar called Luke's: Twelve years ago I sat next to a kid I knew, a hometown punker who went to school at Amherst and, for whatever reason, had shaved his head back to a ten-inch swatch of Mohawk. For odd effect, he had died it hot pink, and as we quietly nursed our beers the heavy-set biker on the next stool studied the kid's hairdo thoughtfully. When he finally stood up to tap my young friend on the shoulder, everything went quiet. Any odds maker in the world would have bet on trouble, but the biker wanted only to know if he could cut himself a two-inch lock to tie a dry fly with.

In September 1805 when Meriwether Lewis and William Clark first encountered a band of Flatheads up the Bitterroot Valley, the Indians had never seen white men before. According to one Indian account, there was "something not quite right" about these travelers, and the fact that the Corps of Discovery sported no blankets led the chiefs to conclude the white men had been robbed somewhere along the way. Captain Clark, for his part, was positive that the gurgling sound of the Flathead language could only mean these Indians were descendants of the mythical lost tribe of Welshmen.

These miscues notwithstanding, the Flathead showed great hospitality to the expedition. Unlike the fierce Blackfeet to the north, the Flathead were so generous and amenable that they soon found themselves in the white men's way, and by 1852 the settlers were obliged to displace them. For the price of $120,000 and a ten-acre tract for each chief, the Flathead were moved from their ancestral home in the Bitterroot Valley and seventy miles to the north.

In 1806, after a rough winter on the coast, Lewis and Clark came tramping back through Montana on their return trip. According to their journals, they bivouacked again at a place near the present-day Montana-Idaho border southwest of town, known as Travelers' Rest (near today's Lolo Hot Springs), and there the two captains split the party, with Clark heading northeast along the route of what the Flathead hunters called the Buffalo Road. Clark was rafting supplies across the river at a "rapid and difficult part of it crouded [sic] with several small islands and willow bars..." when he dumped his raft, drowning his chronometer. Arriving soaking wet on the north bank, he likely continued east, down what is now Main Street. Past the future site of the Union Club Bar, the Adult Entertainment Center, the Taco Bell, and the Fitness Dome, finally entering the narrow canyon later called Hellgate, till he arrived at the Blackfoot River and a trail so prominent that, as the Flathead's Chief Cut-Nose put it, "even a white man could follow it."

I think of what it must have been like to cover the incredible distances the Corps did. While many of us have put in our weekends on these same rivers, the truth is, any bozo can go downstream with his raft and dogs and brewskis. But nobody paddles west against these currents. Nobody bushwhacks, pushes, poles, and drags fully loaded keelboats mile after mile through insect-ridden, rattlesnake-infested, gumbo-clotted Missouri riverbank.

Today locals dote on just about anything to do with Lewis and Clark. People find these accounts inspiring for the sheer understated courage of the adventure, charming for Clark's ingenuous spellings. But mostly I think, people read them because in all their naivety and earnestness, these nineteenth-century adventurers were pretty much dumbstruck—as we all were when we first arrived here. Like a fly in amber, the journals have frozen those moments of awe and barely containable excitement for all time. To this day there are no better-selling books in the area than just about anything to do with Lewis and Clark, who have become namesakes of, among other things, a grade school, a taxidermy studio, and a complete line of bottom-shelf liquors, guaranteed to put you in an exploratory frame of mind.

One hundred ninety years past the Corps of Discovery, I stand at the ground level of my basement window, looking across a backyard that was once prime terrain for the bitterroot, a lily-like flower with a tuberous root. The Flathead mixed this root with berries, mixed it with venison and buffalo jerky, mixed it with about everything they ate. They honored the bitterroot with ritual harvests, celebrated it in ceremonies. Said to be so bitter it could induce nausea, like so many things about this place the bitterroot was definitely an acquired taste. But this near-unpalatable plant with its gorgeous pink flower sustained the Flathead for centuries.

If the great flood cycles of the ice age can be seen as epic, a kind of geological *Gone with the Wind*, then the two-hundred years of Anglo-inflicted change seem speeded up, almost superficial, like some animated feature about termites chewing away at some giant log.

The initial influx of traders and adventurers arriving in the early nineteenth century gave way to the less-nomadic fortune seekers: gold miners, timber barons, and the like—the vanguard of the coming flood of settlers and merchants. Missoula was an emerging town in the American outback, connected to the nation by the Northern Pacific Railroad and eventually by the Milwaukee Road, too. It suffered through the great influenza epidemic in 1915 and then World War I, when Missoula's volunteer rate was 25 percent over what was called for. In terms of casualties, Montana suffered from the highest per capita loss of any state in the union.

But by the end of the Great War, the twentieth century had come to stay, and the frontier days with their renegades and vigilantes were largely a thing of the past, all of which led Jeannette Rankin to observe in a 1970 interview: "People have to conform so much today. In the old days we did what we pleased...."

Twentieth-century Missoula was first a working man's town, a timber town that coexisted with a large university, and this combination would give Missoula a certain earthy gentility. Indeed, for over a century, the timber industry seemed at the heart of Missoula, from the state-of-the-art Smokejumper Center at Johnson Bell Field to the annual Forester's Ball at the University of Montana, where spirited timber beasts sometimes emptied their Colt pistols into the gymnasium ceiling. In the years following World War II, production soared. Loggers razed the Western Montana mountainsides trying to keep up with the unprecedented post-war housing boom. But by the 1970s, about the same time the great Butte copper veins were beginning to bleed out, it occurred to foresters that while it took forty years to grow a timber tree on the coast, it took well over a hundred around here. By the recession of 1982, the timber market took a dive it would never recover from. Mills began to close. Downtown Missoula staggered. The real estate market went down hard and didn't begin to recover till about 1990, when another wave of beleaguered city dwellers began to show up, this time from the West Coast. Many are successful retirees, and many have brought their jobs with them, but the effect has been to boost the price of homes beyond the reach of locals who soldier along with the Missoula economy, the people who have lived here all along.

So at the tail end of the twentieth century, what drives the timber-depleted Missoula economy is the influx of newcomers, some twenty thousand in the last decade. Between the resulting construction bonanza and the accompanying service industries, the boom pretty much feeds itself, but there is no escaping the fact that much of the egalitarianism that used to characterize the town has been misplaced in these transitions, and the other day my neighbor, who has worked for the local paper for twenty years, commented that when he first moved here he was struck by how friendly the place was, something very few of today's immigrants are heard to remark upon.

Now the loggers are disappearing, the miners are under fire, and most of the cowboys I've met want to be poets or maybe screenwriters. In late twentieth-century Missoula, the Corps of Discovery has given way to the Corps of Real Estate. Their pirogues are Chevy Suburbans. Their side arms are their cell phones. Every direction you go, you will find them flogging bits and pieces of the High West to disenchanted Californians and Washingtonians, all hungering for a taste of something pristine. Downtown Missoula reflects these changes with a proliferation of catering services, gourmet kitchenware shops, high-end clothiers, and brokerages. They have changed the face of the downtown, and for the most part (depending on who you talk to) they have changed it for the better, making it a more attractive and livable-looking place.

Like many people, I arrived in Missoula to somehow start my life again. I'd moved west to Colorado in 1977, which was where I first began to hear stories about this fabled town in Montana. A year in the Denver megalopolis gave these stories time to germinate, and finally, the little town up range drew me like a lodestone.

When I arrived here late summer of 1978, Missoula bore little resemblance to what I had imagined. For openers, I had never been to a place with so many running Studebakers. The great bald mountainsides to the east were burnt brown by the powerful summer sun and the

Clark Fork was so low you could walk across it on the cobbles. I marveled at just how dry a place it was. Indeed, the climate seemed not only to have preserved old cars, but also to have mummified much of the sixties counter-culture, so at first Missoula seemed charmingly outdated, the people clannish, eccentric, as if they all shared a joke I may or may not eventually be let in on. The uniqueness of this place caught me off balance. I did not understand that certain Rocky Mountain locutions—"gal" for girl, "crik" for creek—and the odd combination of exhilaration and loneliness the place instilled in me were exactly the things I would grow to cherish.

I moved downtown, right on the river, to a section of Front Street once notorious for its opium dens, roughhouse bars, bordellos, and vigilante justice. Following the disastrous fire of 1892, the neighborhood was gentrified to accommodate a hock shop, a porno theater, two eateries, and a mere handful of bars. In short, Front Street 1978 had about everything a fellow starting over might ever need.

One January night I was sitting on a shockingly decrepit bolster in a bar called the Top Hat. The buttock-piercing springs made me consider capping off the evening with a tetanus shot, one for myself, one for my adventurous girlfriend, Denny. The Missoula Airport was closed for a smog alert and Denny had had to fly into Kalispell, one hundred miles north, then take a Greyhound from there. On the wall beside us in the Top Hat was an amateurish Post-Nuke mural that featured the still-recognizable wreckage of a Missoula laid to ruin. I recall thinking the idea of a nuke strike on Missoula was delusion of grandeur in its purest form. Meanwhile, Denny was losing altitude. She wore a spectacular gold party dress, I wore new pointy-toed cowboy boots. There was nobody else in the place except a three-piece band that seemed to feature an extraordinary lack of talent. They sang countless choruses of a song so obscene, even the title is best left unsaid. It was thirty-three below zero outside, but the valley had finally blown clear. Denny gave me an enlightened kind of look and said, "You know, Fred, you've got a knack for putting yourself in some hellish situations." When we got back to my apartment the pipes were frozen, which did nothing to soften her general stance on the place. And while I thought she was right, I also knew it was my kind of hell—Missoula was.

The next day Denny flew back to Boulder and I stayed on. In addition to my seventy dollar a month apartment over the river, I had secured a kind of "place" for myself along Front Street. I was thirty-four years old and felt I was running out of time. One afternoon I hiked the steep zigzag trail a thousand feet up Mount Sentinel, looked out over the Missoula Valley. The place looked wonderfully, perhaps entrancingly, forlorn. I thought, boy, if there was ever a place for me to make a stand, it would be right here, my back to this mountain. And I came back down the trail as many, perhaps, had done before me, with the resolution that I would change things here, that I would become a writer or die trying. Which sometimes it seems, I very nearly did.

Twenty years later, my two gurus are gone—Hugo is dead, Bill Kittredge has retired. The Front Street I knew in 1978 has morphed again: The porno theater now houses a law firm, the hock shop is a fly-fishing boutique, the infamous Luke's Bar is a catering outfit. The Top Hat is still there, but the new owners have painted over the Post-Nuke mural in eggshell beige.

Today there is no more collectible item around town than the classic Missoula T-shirt. It features a peculiar-looking pot-bellied creature, species undetermined. Neither fish nor fowl, it could be a winged platypus or some kind of big-lipped flying frog. Whatever it is, it glides serenely across the wearer's chest above a logo that states: "Missoula, Montana: A place. Sort of..." In a way, after twenty years of this T-shirt, it still seems to sum up wonderfully the strangely perverse mixture of loyalty and annoyance the place inspires, the dark humor, self-deprecation, and fierce pride this town is capable of producing among its residents.

Missoula is a town that makes demands on you. With its pristine backdrop and its scrim of emissions, with its nationally-ranked writing program and rock-bottom faculty salaries, with its speculator's housing market and embattled economic base, Missoula is a place you have to want to stay.

But when Missoula opens its smoky old heart in the summer, we will forgive it just about anything. In summer it seems the whole town moves outside. The clear mountain air cools 40 degrees at night and dries your sweat. The languorous twilights with their parfait of colors linger on and on, like some well-loved dinner guest.

I've heard it said Missoula is a great place to come back to, and that may be right. Recent studies have shown that a substantial percentage of the people moving in are actually Montana returnees—people who moved away to acquire a better job, training, or skills—and who have now moved back better prepared to deal with the region's economic challenges. Personally I've returned here twice—after a sojourn east, and one west. My wife and I—whom I met, incidentally, in Richard Hugo's poetry workshop—now have two young children and a thirty-year mortgage, so it's unlikely we will be leaving again anytime soon. Certainly it's easy to imagine a place where the economy is more supportive, where the living's not quite so hard. But it's impossible to find a place that's so much fun as this one—with auroras in the night sky, wilderness at your doorstep, and these great, green rivers with their rushing dreams of flood.

And these mountains—lumpish and un-heroic, the ones that block the morning sun—these mountains come alive in evening, when they seem to absorb the twilight, to grow and shift, to morph into great mysterious shapes, like the pyramids, but older. A friend once said they're like a huge drive-in screen, where if you watch closely, the secrets of the place are revealed. If you watch closely and you watch faithfully, you may learn that this is a place with a preternatural ability to reinvent itself, over and over.

Rebel with a Pacemaker

On July 4, 1947, William "Wino Willie" Forkner, Dionysus of the Harley-Davidson, led members of Los Angeles's Booze Fighters Motorcycle Club on a ride north and into the annals of American folk lore when they turned the drowsy streets of Hollister, California into a combination beer blast and raceway. It was thirty-six hours of thrills, spills and cycle hijinx for some, a nightmare on wheels for others, but the incident would go on to inspire the Marlon Brando classic, *The Wild One* and with it, a whole generation of outlaw biker wannabes.

Fifty years later, July 4, 1997, Hollister's Granada theater was showing *The Wild One* around the clock. Before you even had your morning huevos, you could walk into the air-conditioned darkness and, for fifty cents, see the smoldering young Brando knock heads with his arch rival (played by Lee Marvin), the leader of a motorcycle club called, oddly enough, The Beetles.

But the moment everyone waits for is when Brando is pressed to answer the big question:

What are you guys rebelling against, anyway?

Brando pouts for a second, then mumbles his fabled response, "Whad'ya got?" At which point the audience at the Granada, comprised entirely of bikers, goes wild.

At the foot of the Diablo mountains, Hollister (population twenty thousand) seems like a town right out of a Steinbeck novel. The apricot and cherry orchards begin right at the city limits. Some residents, particularly the seniors, questioned the wisdom of an event celebrating the fiftieth anniversary of what was widely viewed as the mugging of their town. Nevertheless, the event went on as scheduled, was even billed as "California's Biggest Rally Ever," though before a permit was granted, the promoters had to agree to forty-two conditions, including a private security force, a fenced function site, and a five-million-dollar bond.

Still, only about forty-thousand bikers attended, less than half of the anticipated crowds. Parading up and down San Benito Street, the cyclists blipped their throttles, slipped their clutches, gobbled up the souvenir T-shirts, pins, posters, and other memorabilia in an attempt, it seemed, to grab a tangible piece of a somewhat intangible moment. As always, the motorcycles were spectacular. About ninety percent of them were Harleys and, at fifteen thousand dollars per ride, there was maybe sixty million dollars worth of machinery, rolling around in very close quarters. Needless to say, the riders were restrained.

Maybe it was because of the heightened security and media scrutiny, but the rally felt vaguely self-conscious, reduced to a bare-bones kind of narcissism. As they rode, many of the bikers wore a meditative expression as if it might yet come to them what, exactly, they were here for.

In the meantime, other kinds of things came to the forefront. For example, there was the Playboy pavilion, featuring its unique brand of fantasy—as always, a perfect balance between the absurd and the unattainable: a forty-thousand-dollar custom Harley, straddled by Playmates in outfits almost comically revealing, outfits that seemed part Rocky Horror Show, part Hooter's uniform, part Jeremiah Johnson's coming out party. Still, the fact that an upscale mag like Playboy is doing business at a traditionally blue collar event like a motorcycle rally speaks volumes about the kinds of people buying big motorcycles these days.

And then there were the Hell's Angels, who arrived early to stake out the back of Johnny's Bar. Even the long term president of the Oakland chapter showed up, and at the height of the event. People lined up twelve deep for the privilege of drinking a three-dollar cup of Bud in this august company, though the Angels did not attend the events of 1947. In fact, in 1947 the Angels did not yet exist.

The Boozefighters, on the other hand, were there in 1947, and Wino Willie bears as much resemblance to Sonny Barger as Buddy Holly does to, say, Iggy Pop.

BFMC was essentially a racing fraternity, and the members prided themselves on competing in weekend races on the same bikes they rode to work every day. The name seems to have been chosen for the simple reason that it was outrageous, though there is little argument that BFMC liked to play very hard, then party very hardy—kind of a rugby club on wheels. Willie reveled in his reputation as the original Wild One (The Lee Marvin character was modeled closely after him), but he seemed baffled by the reputation for violence and mayhem the later clubs were so anxious to cultivate, and by their open contempt for all bikes not American: "Hell, I don't care what kind of bike you ride or even whether you drink or not," Willie once stated. "You're still a Bro to me."

The original Boozefighter "colors" were not bought for five hundred dollars a pop in some cycle boutique, and they were not outlaw black. In fact, they were kelly green, mostly because that happened to be the shade of the sale-priced sweaters Willie found at Sears.

Before the events of 1947, his claim to fame was the time in 1946 when a well-oiled Willie crashed the fence at El Cajon Speedway. With the crowd cheering him on, he out-rode the pack of flabbergasted racers for a full three laps before he put his 1933 Indian into a fence. "Who cares about goin' to jail if you leave people smilin'?" Willie once said, and it seems he lived this credo to the end.

Maybe the void at Hollister was caused by the absence of spirits such as Wino Willie, who passed away days before the event. Willie was not pre-packaged anything...

Maybe, in the end, it was a sense of joy that was missing, a sense that any of this might somehow be fun. Maybe it's the relentless selling, the idea that this can only be fun if you have your life savings invested in a "fantasy" bike. Or if Playboy Magazine is there to show you how. Often, amid all the million-dollar lifestyle packaging, posturing and general bad-assery, the idea that motorcycling is supposed to be fun seems to have been all but forgotten.

The Guggenheim's Art
of the Motorcycle

June 24, 1998: A platoon of media folk jostle each other anxiously. Soon there is the rumble of approaching motorcycles; specifically, large displacement, twin-cylinder jobs. By turns ominous and exciting, the sound of the old-concept big twin still has the sheer visceral appeal of hoofbeats, thunder, drum solos. The newer, faster 4-cylinder jobs sound mostly like bumble bees. A couple of frontrunners herald the arrival of the pack—about a hundred cyclists thunder in, brake to a crawl, blip their throttles, nose their machines curbside, so that, finally, the entire block, both sides, is wall-to-wall bikes, much in the manner of those fabled cycle events at Sturgis or Daytona Beach.

But wait, what's this? There's no beer tent, bikini bike-wash, or poker run, none of the traditional biker Bacchanalia in evidence here. Nobody named Filthy Phil, Wino Willie, or Big Fun, as far as I can tell. In fact, many of

them have names like Wilhelm and Klaus, as this cycle-
cade is comprised entirely of BMW motorcycles arriving
from the Manhattan BMW dealership on Fifty-Seventh
Street. More important, we're not at some Biker Mardi
Gras. Of all places, we're at the Guggenheim Museum on
Park Avenue for an exhibit called, "The Art of The Motorcycle." Sponsored by BMW, it is a premiere display of
motorcycles, past and present. Right there on that august
ramp where the Monets and Cézannes used to hang, there
now perch raucous, hooligan motorcycles; Beezers and
Triumphs, Guzzis, Harleys, and an Indian Chief, all sitting there bold as brass, like so many oil-dripping *objets
d'art*.

It's close to 90 degrees by the time the press and riders disengage, repair to the museum. Those sporting full
leathers are sweating mightily. A quick spin through the
Guggenheim doors and suddenly it seems so quiet, not to
say hushed, perhaps even sanctified in that cool, lofty gallery. Plus it is infused with the brilliant yet mellifluous light
I generally associate with the Outer Body Experience. As
soon as you walk in, front and center in the rotunda is the
entire arc of the motorcycle's evolution, distilled down to
two machines: an 1868 Michaux Perreaux, a pumped-
up buggy-like contraption with barrel-stave wheels and
a miniature steam engine that looks like a sleeping bag
wrapped with a venetian blind. A few paces away sits a
1998 Italian-built MV F 4, a bike that looks more like
a fighter-plane, capable of speeds approaching 200 miles
per hour. World renowned architect Frank Gehry designed the installation, which features raw lumber and
a kind of stainless steel möbius along the rampway, the
mirror-like surfaces working to provide an ongoing conversation between the past and present.

As you ascend the ramp, the whimsical clunkiness of the old Daimlers and Majestics gradually morphs away into the sleeker, more sophisticated machines, and by the time you wind your way to the top, there is the very latest 1200cc muscle-blue Buell, a kind of hybrid Harley that seems to look less like a machine and more like a piece of future-sculpture, one that is perhaps entitled "Escape Velocity."

Curious thing, the motorcycle. Robert Pirsig (*Zen and the Art of Motorcycle Maintenance*) calls it the "chariot of the soul." This is probably true because, besides packing your soul off down the highway, these machines have precious few practical applications. So, to paraphrase Melissa Pierson, another writer/rider, what the hell is it about these machines?

Well, for openers, there are the names; the Guggenheim exhibit features bikes with such marvelous names as the Flying Merkel, the Solex Velosolex, and the Aeramachi Chimera. There is the Elf, the Beta Techno, and my personal favorite, The Scott Squirrel Sprint Special.

Then, of course, there is the sheer variety of bikes. This exhibit claims there have been over 3,400 different makes in a little over a hundred years. So it would seem that everybody and his dog feels moved to build a better Chariot of the Soul. What's more, it's like the very idea of inventing a motorcycle taps into some ancient, lizard-brain center of pre-adolescent fantasy, the one that would blend the body with the machine, and as you climb the ramp, what you end up seeing is an endless permutation of dream machines with motors of every possible configuration. Some of these bikes have wonderful smooth flowing lines, some are almost comic, some are shark-like, menacing. Some are all business—jet-black and alloy, some seem painted up to look like goat carts or even May baskets.

"The Art of the Motorcycle" features all the greats: the exotics, like the Megola and that fabulous Czech bike, the Bohmerland. There are the warp-speed Japanese bikes, a wonderful selection of antique American iron that includes a Curtis V-8, an Iver-Johnson V-twin, and a 1939 Crocker. Of course, there are those legendary Brits, the Brough Superior, Matchless, and Sunbeam. But as always, no machine commands more attention than the deco-inspired, post-war Indian Chief. The 1940's Chiefs are a wonderful combination of the preposterous and the fabulous. With their huge, valanced fenders, hand-shifts, and Indian-red paint jobs, they are machines straight out of a young boy's dream: equal parts cow pony, fire-breathing dragon, and mechanical wizardry—the very incarnation of every childhood fantasy of speed, power, and flight I ever had. And maybe not just me—for of all the marvelous machines on that ramp, the Chief was most heavily photographed of them all.

A short way up the ramp you encounter the central thesis of this exhibit in the form of the following test (written on the wall):

"The motorcycle is a metaphor for the twentieth century. Invented by a French engineer, the motorcycle has tracked the great themes of the modern era...fantasy, romance, rebellion, danger and freedom are states of being that have been projected on its evolving form since the notion of mechanized personal transport first emerged..."

This is heady stuff. It's probably even true. What's more, the time I spent on the Guggenheim ramp caused me to think in upwardly spiraling terms. Perhaps it even caused me to attempt huge, even ungainly leaps of intuition. For example, if it's true we are experiencing the legitimization/rediscovery of motorcycles, I would like to point to a potent coincidence: the parallel legitimization/ rediscovery of cigars.

After I left the Guggenheim I stopped for a beer at a downtown bar. In the beery afternoon sunlight a group of young swells, dressed like their granddads in white shirts and braces, puffed away like lord's bastards on panatellas as big as their heads. For all the notions of ascent and escape velocity, I thought, well, right there is your continuum. Bikes and cigars, cigars and bikes. They're both expensive. They're both hazardous to your health. They're big and smelly. And they're hard to keep going.

Bikes and cigars. You may not think they're pretty. You may not think they're art. You love them or you hate them but they're plainly here to stay.

2002

Under the Rapids

In the bow, my grown-up son paddles right beside me. His big sister paddles in the seat just behind. It occurs to me the three of us form the raft's spearhead, whatever that might mean. Kyle is a computer graphics guy, living in New York. He's a rangy, athletic young man, relaxed and catlike in temperament. My daughter Sara works for a family resources organization, also in New York. She is dark eyed, dark haired. When she chooses, she can unleash a smile bright as the North Star. At a guess, right now I'd say there is something on her mind. Since her arrival I've watched her attention flow, ebb, disappear completely, and then she seems to drop right out of the moment. I know this tic when I see it, because it's something I do myself.

I have another pair of children, Kyle and Sara's half-siblings. They are three decades younger, still tots and home with their mom. In the stern of the raft is Brianna, the petite rock-jock undergrad who has babysat my new kids since they were infants. Brianna's friend Dave is our river guide, and nearly as I can figure, Dave is guiding this outing because he has a hopeless crush on Brianna, who looks charming indeed with her cropped raven hair and jet-black suit.

All this is to say it's pretty close quarters in this raft; it seems packed with familials in various real and imagined configurations. In recognition of this fact, I suppose, we all crack a Bud.

In 1974, after their mom remarried, I left Kyle and Sara to embark on a ten-year series of false starts, wanderings, and misadventures. I did not see my daughter again till 1984. I did not see my son again till 1996. Throughout my sabbatical, the possibility of a reunion such as the raft trip we're on was both a lodestone and a thing to dread. At the time, I did not really want anyone to know me. At the time, I could barely stand to know myself.

So we're new to all this, my grown children and I. We only barely know each other, and this raft trip has about it a real shakedown quality.

There's not a lot of talking in the rapids. Really, the closest you come to conversation is to try and paddle in synch, so we lumber along down this rioting green serpentine beneath this brilliant July sky, doing the best we can to keep it all afloat.

The runoff's been heavy. There's some big damn water here and everyone knows it. To my understanding, one school of thought says the river is actually safer this way, that the rapids are "washed out" with all but the biggest rocks buried. The other school says the extra volume of water simply masks the hazards. I ask our gorge guide, Dave, which school he subscribes to. "Both," he says, and gives me a What, Me Worry? kind of grin, one that inspires, simultaneously, both confidence and misgiving. He casts a radiant glance at Brianna in her hot black suit. So, for that matter, does Kyle. Dave scowls at the way my son and I are paddling, which is to say without much enthusiasm, and he says, "Hey you guys up front. Quit that damn lily dipping."

Kyle and I drain our Buds, crumple our cans, try to paddle with more conviction "Wow," says Kyle, shaking his head. "To be caught lily dipping. I'm mortified."

There are seven sets of rapids in this Class 3 section of the Clark Fork, where something like 32,000 cubic feet of water per second surge along a six-mile stretch. They still bear the colorfully life-threatening monikers given to them by the earliest boatmen: "Boateater," "Tumbleweed," "Fang."

We breeze through Tumbleweed, power through the set they call Boateater, and when we're safely through, I tell my daughter, "Not to bring you down, Sara, but a rafter ate it going through here just a couple weeks ago."

I am not sure what I'm thinking, introducing this particular information. Maybe I mean to add piquancy to our outing. Maybe I mean it as a distraction. Maybe it's just that, years ago, a friend passed on similar information to me in the course of a big-wall rock climb. Something about his casual handling of matters of high seriousness has appealed to me ever since. I knew my friend wasn't trying to frighten me. He was simply telling me that it was necessary to tread as carefully as we could.

But today on the river, it doesn't work like it should. Sara regards me with amusement, then bafflement, then dismissal. The way this caveat works today, it's like I've proclaimed that having shot the killer rapids the worst is over.

For a few seconds Dave holds us in the current above

the single cuspid-looking rock known as Fang while he figures our approach. When he tells us "go," I hook my foot tight in the raft's stirrup and we dig in hard with our paddles. There's a sudden jerk and our raft is borne on a huge upswell as we head directly for the bright roaring mass before us. Instantly I am in the water.

There's not a lot to do under the rapids. Everything is dark, quiet. I want to say "serene," but that's not quite right. But the forces are so powerful your body shuts down, so you just tumble along the bottom like a large sodden basketball. The light grows brighter, then dimmer, then brighter again. I watch the hard silver bubbles shoot through the surging green while I wonder, in an abstract kind of way, exactly how long a human being can reasonably expect to stay alive, twelve feet under in fifty-degree water. But mostly, I wonder if there's someone with me down there, and if there is, if it's one of my children. And if so, how bad a fix we're in.

Finally, my life jacket flings me upward and I surface ten feet from Sara. Her eyes are wild and dilated, her mouth is gasping, her chest heaving. We breach the water in such perfect synchronicity that the mirroring effect is incredible.

I swim over to her—swim as much as one does in the rapids with a cumbersome life jacket around one's neck—reach her in short order, wrap my arms around her. "I've got you, Sara," I tell her. "I've got you. I've got you," and it strikes me I've waited an awfully long time to tell her this, and it's a curious little moment, joyful and desperate all at once. Because while it's true that I am hanging on to her, if anyone's got us, it's the rapids.

By the time we reach calmer water, the raft finally catches up. From the stern, Dave pulls Sara back on board while my strong-armed son yanks me up over the bow, lands me like a halibut, gasping and panting in the brilliant sunlight.

"Wow," our guide observes, with genuine admiration. "You guys were down there a long time…"

We crack a lot of macho jokes, take to the shore for lunch; the trip continues with unabated dodging-the-bullet kind of merriment. In the evening Brianna does double duty, babysitting my little ones while their mother and I explore the city's taverns with Kyle and Sara, where our gorge adventure is fodder for the family mythology. And yet, from the moment Sara and I broke the surface together, I'm fixated with the idea that, beyond the fact we survived, something extraordinary happened.

It is months before I get Sara's letter. As I read it, I understand that throughout our re-acquaintance she has made attempts to prepare me for it. Yet I am unprepared, nonetheless. The letter describes a ten-year span of darkness and confusion in her life that ran contiguous, an exact parallel to my own. I won't reveal the nature of it. But like the rapids, the letter took my breath away. Like the rapids, the letter was too powerful to struggle with, and it pummeled me blithely along till it was finished with me, till it finally released me to the light.

Remember my old rock climbing friend's caveat that starts, "Not to bring you down…"? The one about treading lightly? It's worth mentioning here that long ago he failed to take his own advice. He grew careless (we'll never know quite how) and lost his life in exactly the same spot he meant long ago to alert me to. If you like ironies, it's a great one. But like a double negative, a cautionary tale about a cautionary tale seems to cancel itself out. Maybe the same goes for metaphors—how many of them, in the end, can we stand to make? We want so badly to learn from, to connect up all this life experience, to examine, reexamine, and exorcize it. But maybe enough is finally enough.

So while our family raft trip, our submarine journeys and re-emergences, plumbed the experiential depths, mostly I'm thinking how great it is—just to survive. In fact, maybe survival is one of the great underrated pleasures in life. To learn to hang on and hang on, to learn to treasure those people you come so close to losing. To simply live to tell the story—maybe that's all the trip was about after all.

The Lost Tribe of Indian

On November 1, 2003, I flew to Los Angeles to attend a "support rally" for the second incarnation of an American legend. Defunct since 1953, the fabled Indian Motorcycle Company was kick-started back to life in 1999. But four years later it found itself, once again, on the verge of extinction.

Organized by the Indian Riders Group, the twenty dollar support rally buy-in included a T-shirt, rally pin, and a twelve-mile ride from Indian's flagship dealership in Laguna Beach to the Peterson Automotive Museum in Hollywood.

By one o'clock, hundreds of second-generation Indians were thundering up the ramp to the Peterson's rooftop parking lot. Manufactured in Gilroy, a four hours' ride north, the new Indians were spectacular in ensemble: multihued, graceful, and powerful looking. In contrast to the vintage (or "first generation") rallies I've attended, there wasn't a gray beard or leaky old bike to be seen. Indeed, these riders were mostly strapping, workingman types in their twenties and thirties. On arrival they greeted each other warmly, arranged their bikes for the cameras, swapped the latest gossip about the embattled company's prospects. But when deposed CEO Frank O'Connell rose to address them, they fell immediately silent.

Slight, close-cropped, and fiftyish, the former Reebok executive managed to look almost preppie in his riding leathers, and began his remarks tentatively: "As you all know, Indian Motorcycles closed its doors six weeks ago."

The crowd drew a breath.

"The company's now for sale, and we're currently entertaining bidders. We have not yet declared bankruptcy, but it does remain an option..."

O'Connell surveyed the anxious faces. He seemed pleased by the turnout, pained by the occasion.

"It's great to be here with you today," he continued. "Because we all know these bikes are not just pieces of metal. That it's a...a spiritual thing to ride them, and that it can't stop now."

His voice broke.

"It just can't. We've all come too far...so thanks for the support, and let's hope there's a way for us to go on from here."

There was light applause, plenty of murmuring. It's hard to say exactly what this crowd was looking for. But if it was Moses, come down from the mountain, they sure didn't get it.

In a few minutes I went over to speak to O'Connell, and found him fending off the questions of a Harley-riding motor press journalist known as "Super-Glide Gail."

"So," said Gail, in total hardball mode. "I'm thinking these new bikes of yours are basically Harley clones tricked out to look like Indians. Is that pretty much why you guys went under?"

Though her timing couldn't have been worse, Gail had managed to put her finger right on the second-generation Indian's biggest problem, which was one of credibility.

In the course of his IMC tenure, O'Connell must have fielded this question hundreds of times, and he responded patiently, almost dreamily that while in some ways the new Indians resembled Harley-Davidson, Indian designers had assiduously and painstakingly made them different enough to earn Original Equipment Manufacturer (OEM) status in 2002, and that whatever resemblance might still remain was now, for a whole variety of reasons, a totally moot point.

Meanwhile, a catering truck pulled in and a sumptuous Mexican buffet was set up on folding tables in the concourse. But before the crowd could descend upon it, a black rider stood on a tabletop and offered a benediction: "In the Bible, it says that 'Where there is no Spirit, the people must perish,'" he began.

As examples of people who had such spirit, the rider cited Black Elk, Mahatma Gandhi, and Martin Luther King, but stopped well short of including Frank O'Connell. When the moment ran its course, the rider then proposed a moment of prayer and invoked the gathering to "all join hands."

The crowd seemed tentative.

"Come on, you guys," he entreated. "This is tough on all of us. Let's reach out and touch somebody."

"No way, man," muttered a heavyset rider. "This here's West Hollywood."

Still, it's not every day your bike goes extinct right out from under you and, after an awkward minute, the group of riders gradually took each others' hands, and on a rooftop lot in the heart of Los Angeles, proceeded with great dignity to pray for the survival of Indian Motorcycles.

Ontologically speaking, the Peterson Rally might seem a spectacularly unlikely event—unless you've ever poured heart and soul into such a machine.

My own story began in 1996 when I undertook the restoration of a post-war Indian from a large box of parts known as a "basket case." In the throes of midlife burnout, the fact that my project and I were both in our fifties lent a curious urgency to it, and the deeper my involvement got, the more convinced I was that I would find answers there. In eighteen months' time, with the help of biker friends and mechanical aptitude I'd not known I possessed, I'd rebuilt a fringed and studded, vintage 1947 Chief in dazzling midnight blue. Wherever I rode, my ride turned heads, but beyond this, the process seemed to precipitate a joyous and surprising string of events, for along with the bike came a new baby, and with that, a new outlook and, in short order, a book about these adventures, *Rebuilding the Indian*, that ultimately brought me to what was likely the first ever book-signing event the great Sturgis Motorcycle Rally ever hosted. In this way it was easy to see my life in two phases: Before the Indian and After.

I didn't know it at the time, but in this sort of thinking I'd gained membership to a particularly crusty tribe of Indian zealots, most of us old enough to have seen these bikes in their heyday. For years, we ate, slept, and breathed old Indians, trailered our restorations around to "Indian Days" rallies, swapped maintenance tips like banana bread recipes at Bridge Club. We had these bikes to ourselves for so long, we became like those stalwart monks that kept Christianity alive through the dark ages. We were the keepers of the Indian Faith, and as such, authorities on whatsoever was Real, and whatsoever was Fake.

There was something special about these bikes, right from their beginning. The Indian was designed in 1901 by Norwegian immigrant Oskar Hedstrom, a year before the birth of Harley-Davidson. The similarity of their large-bore V-twin engines somehow inflamed brand loyalties, and the two marques grew up through America's motor adolescence the bitterest sibling rivals. If Indian stroked its motor, Harley followed suit. If Harley had a new trans-mission, then Indian made one, too. Always slightly faster, Indian posted speed and endurance records Harley chased for years. And in style, there was no machine to match the full-dress Indian Chief. With its graceful valanced fenders and brilliant color schemes, there is an innocence, an exu-berance about these bikes that is almost touching. Tricked out with enough studs, fringe and frippery to belong in a Hopalong Cassidy movie, the seventy-four-cubic-inch postwar Chiefs were a wonderful blend of the preposter-ous and the fabulous: equal parts cow pony, fire-breath-ing dragon, and mechanical wizardry, and when Indian Motorcycle went bankrupt in 1953, these bikes became instant classics.

Quickly, the Indian marque was snatched up by Eng-land's robust Associated Motorcycles Group, who for the next five years marketed their British-made bikes in this country using the Indian nameplate.

It was all terribly confusing, but it only got worse: In the next few decades, a succession of crackpots and rip-off artists worked the bereaved Indian faithful like third-rate mediums. Conjuring Indian "prototypes" out of pot-metal and duct-tin, they conned thousands of believers by the promise of, as one hustler put it, "the return of an American icon."

These scams happened so regularly, you'd think the fans would get wise. Yet so potent was the idea of an Indian revival that by 1998—forty-five years after they quit the business—the defunct Indian marque still managed to sell $26 million in worthless stock and nonexistent bikes. Such blind and unwavering faith made us restorers incredibly cynical, yet it also managed to bring about the first "serious" revival attempt yet mounted.

Finally, by the late 1990s, Denver attorney Rick Block thought to assemble dozens of Indian rip-off claims into a $16 million receivership, the idea being that whoever wished to use the trademark henceforth should have to first pay off the debt. Of all who would contend for it, perhaps the least likely was Canadian entrepreneur Murray Smith, who had just purchased a growing Canadian concern called the Indian Manufacturing Company. Contrary to what the name implied, Indian Manufacturing actually produced an extensive, Hilfiger-style line of sportswear— over three hundred items ranging from windbreakers to camisoles, all bearing the distinctive retro script and war bonnet logo of the late great Indian Motorcycle Company. Despite the fact Indian hadn't made a bike since the Korean War, Indian Manufacturing Company was worth a cool $16 million when Smith bought it in 1997. He figured if a defunct American icon could sell that many BVDs, it didn't have to stop there. In fact, Smith became so convinced of its marketing potential, he envisioned a billion-dollar global "Lifestyle Brand," one that would go head to head with Harley-Davidson's. In this incarnation the resurrected Indian marque would include not just motorcycles, but also such products as cigars, aftershave, bottled water, oxygen bars, and a chain of bistros modeled after the Hard Rock Café.

But there was a hitch: To prevent the chronic, pie-in-the-sky fraud long associated with Indian revival attempts in the past, prospective buyers were required to demonstrate not only their fiscal accountability—they were also required to produce the kind of feasible, viable, bona fide motorcycle design that had long been sorely lacking.

To come up with such a design quickly, Smith would need somebody who knew a tailpipe from a tank top. To this end, he engaged the talents of Rey Sotelo, a California-based builder of high-end custom Harley-Davidsons. With receivership proceedings just a few months away, Sotelo dove into the project headfirst. Using $50,000 worth of aftermarket Harley parts, fabricated sheet metal, and Indian badging, in eight weeks' time he created a stunning black and red modern Chief, a bike that was not only faithful to the traditional Indian lines, not only plausible in appearance, but one that was drop-dead gorgeous to boot. Sotelo's bike was not a mock-up or a design "on the page," but a bike that you could ride right into a federal courtroom, if only such things were allowed.

Talk about a winning argument. According to one account, presiding judge Vita Wineshank was so taken by Sotelo's handiwork that she actually came down off the bench herself to swing a leg over it and hop on board.

Sotelo, at least, was under no illusions about what he'd done. There's a huge difference between building a single "replica" bike and the creation of a genuine, Original Equipment Manufacturer (OEM) revival. But Sotelo's motorcycle was so convincing, so thoroughly Indian looking that the next day Murray Smith, haberdasher and visionary, wrote a check to the Colorado Federal Claims

Court for $26 million. The Indian marque was his, free and clear.

Now came the hard part.

Early in 1999 the rejuvenated Indian Motorcycle Company, formerly of Springfield, Massachusetts, set up shop in a converted garlic processing plant in Gilroy, California, not far from the San Andreas Fault. Flushed with success, the new company pledged, as many had before, to reinstate a true American classic. But the honeymoon was short.

In its first year, IMC built 2,500 motorcycles, but what the buyers were getting was essentially the same Harley-powered "kit bike" (a bike comprised of aftermarket parts) that Sotelo had rolled into the courtroom the year before. Cycling press and public alike were most unkind. For many, an Indian motorcycle with a Harley-designed motor was more than a disappointment—it was an anomaly akin to a Ford-powered Corvette.

By the end of 1999, with increasing public skepticism, Indian Motorcycle needed to move quickly toward a proprietary motor, yet the board of directors was deadlocked on how best to proceed. On the one hand, Murray Smith thought the estimated $250 million needed for the Indian's OEM motor should be generated by his "lifestyle brand" paraphernalia.

Other board members disagreed. They felt they had enough on their hands just reviving the motorcycle, that the OEM funding should come from going public. After much dispute, it was decided that Smith would complete an IPO offering that fall. Unhappily, the board postponed their offering in hopes the booming pre-millennial market would rise even higher. With the collapse of 2000, the newly reborn Indian Motorcycle Company was in trouble.

Eventually, Indian turned to the Massachusetts-based investment group, Audax, for the much-needed cash infusion. Audax was good for $100 million—but only pending Indian's complete corporate overhaul, and there followed in Gilroy a period of major transition that one disgruntled worker characterized this way: "The blue jeans all left, and the suits came to stay."

Still, another two years would pass before Indian finally delivered a one hundred-cubic-inch, high-performance proprietary motor they called "the PowerPlus." Redesigned around this engine, the 2002 Chiefs finally had an OEM motor to go with their retro-pizzazz styling. The new Indians were fast, elegant, powerful. After stumbling badly, they seemed finally to have their own motorcycle, and by 2002 orders were coming in, production was ramping up, and the motor press was beginning to take them seriously.

Up to this point, these new Indians were easy to dismiss. Many was the cocktail party where I damned them with a sniff and the following line: "They're not a real Indian—they're a custom EVO motor on a soft-tail frame."

And yet. There was something subversive about IMC's latest efforts. From all accounts, these new Indians ran great. What's more, they looked right. But mostly, the new Indians managed to sow seeds of doubt that my 1947 Chief was really enough fun.

In point of fact, the whole vintage experience had become a bit shopworn for me. Everyone knows that vintage Indians are the ultimate Real Deal bike. They are handsome, proud, and studly, much like having a super cool dad. Yet five years past my restoration and its accompanying Feel Good themes, there had come the inevitable back-swell of reality.

Many is the ride I've failed to take simply because my

vintage bike wouldn't run. Sometimes it was a glitch—a short circuit or bad battery—and sometimes it was more serious, like a leaky gas tank. I find its cold-start drill as intricate and unforgiving as a sobriety test, while a total mastery of its left-hand throttle and "suicide" tank-shift remains as elusive and unrewarding a proposition as mirror writing or Esperanto. If my vintage Chief was indeed a kind of metaphor for getting on with your life, well— it wasn't the kind of metaphor you rode very far from home.

Gradually, in my mind, the sepia-toned ambience of my 1947 Chief was being eclipsed by the sheer excess of these new Chiefs, which were big and shiny, fast, scary, and larger than life. Movies stars had discovered these bikes. Schwarzenegger even ran his into the back of a city bus. Once again, Indians were happening. And if my 1947 Chief was a leisurely putt down memory lane, with twice the horsepower the new Indians were a screaming, bat-out-of-hell run down some shimmering, existential black-top.

By June 2003 I could stand it no longer. I called Indian publicist Martin Hendess, (an Audax-appointed MBA from Villanova) and asked him for a demo bike.

"But you write about vintage Indians," he said.

"Yeah. But now I want to write about a new one."

"Wow. Well. What do you want to write about it?"

"I dunno—I haven't ridden it yet"

"But you will write about it?"

"Hell yes, Martin. If I can ride one, I'll write about it."

And so it happened that on a sweltering evening last August, when the air was blue with forest fire smoke, an enormous high-rise semi crept up our quiet Missoula street and rolled to a stop. The truck—a brand-new, snow white Kenworth—was so big, it rendered toy-like the modest bungalows of our neighborhood. Painted on its cab was a winged grand piano, and a rolling flight of keys unfurled along its oversize trailer.

The driver bounded out. He was young, ginger haired, clad in shorts. He punched a button at the back of the trailer, lowered the hydraulic lift to the pavement.

I glanced at my five-year-old son. We were waiting for a motorcycle, not a piano, so we must have looked perplexed.

The driver climbed aboard the gate, grinned at us. "You guys coming up or not?" he said.

The three of us rose grandly to the trailer door. The driver unlatched it briskly, opened it with a flourish.

A scrim of road dust hung briefly in the air, and there was a pungent Pharaoh-scent of cedar chips and high-priced lacquer. It was dark as a tar bucket back there, but when our eyes adjusted, we caught a flash of chrome, a wink of headlight glass coming from between two Steinway crates way to the front. The three of us made our way toward it.

It was hard to get a good look in that gloom, but the bike sat upright, strapped to a wheeled pallet something like a skateboard. I helped the driver, a moonlighting journalism student, slide crates around to make a path. He told us that his company's forte was prestige pianos, but that sometimes motorcycles rode shotgun to fill up a load.

"Big bikes and concert grands?" I said.

The driver shrugged. "My boss—he's a total cycle freak."

We locked the pallet wheels down, gently ferried the big machine back toward the lift gate in the back.

By now, kids, passersby, and neighbors had gathered to

see what was up, and when the bike finally emerged, there was a faint, collective gasp.

"That's no piano," someone finally whispered.

Glistening there beneath the street lights, poised to descend, was a hulking, coal black, fringed, dressed, and studded Indian PowerPlus Chief, a machine that for all practical purposes had been extinct for fifty years.

Looking back, what impressed me most was that the bike came with no manual, license plates, or instructions of any kind. What impressed my son most was the fact there was no kick-starter. He had yet to learn bikes could have electric starting.

When we'd landed on the ground, I climbed on the bike to steady it while the driver released the tie-down straps.

I thought Tobin's point—that there was no apparent way to start it—was well-taken: Beyond the fact it had two wheels, the Black Chief resembled my 1947 Chief about the way an F-16 does a biplane. But I managed to roll it away without incident while the driver stored the lift. The bike felt long, wide, and slightly top-heavy.

"Crank it up!" someone said.

"Yeah, See what it's got!"

They weren't exactly suggestions. Wow, I thought. What a tough crowd! For me to ride this bike without a clue was almost too dumb for words. And yet, with an entrance like this, I somehow had no choice.

The driver grinned, showed me the starting drill. In a moment, the bike idled robustly beneath me while I sat and blipped the throttle like a boob.

The driver cocked his head: "You do have a valid cycle permit. Don't you?"

I'd been meaning to get one of these for some time—about eight years to be exact. For a moment I was sure he knew this, but I said: "Of course! Jesus! Are you out of your mind?"

With that I slipped the clutch, bumped off the curb, blasted off through the worst fire season Montana's ever had, just as fast as I could go. I downshifted badly for a traffic light, sailed through the yellow, then tweaked the throttle hard. Holy Jesus, I thought. My face is flying off! This is what's been missing!

Within weeks of the Black Chief's arrival—about the time it took for me to stop riding like an idiot—I got an e-mail from Hendess with a one word message: "Argh!" Website down, the phones disconnected, the new Indian had gone under with barely a whimper, leaving in my garage a peculiar kind of orphan—one of the biggest, most expensive, and suddenly, most collectible cruiser bikes in the world.

It was much to ponder. Amid my garage's clutter of skis, mowers, shotguns, snow tires (basically none of the things you'd see in the kind of upscale garage this bike was obviously meant to sit in), the Black Chief sat in kickstand limbo. For the moment, it belonged nowhere—not with me, not with a dealer, not with the factory.

I found these events had a double-edged effect: First, there was morbid fascination. It took Indian fifty years to get out of hock, five years to claw their way back into the market, and yet they still managed to blow it! It was the exquisite, cut-your-throat style of falling short only a Red Sox fan could fathom.

Second, there was a ghoulish kind of excitement. I thought there was an excellent chance that this particular press bike, so far away from home and in the midst of such chaos, would somehow fall through the cracks and become my own.

My cycling friends were quick to lend advice: "Move it out of state!"

"Tell 'em it's been stolen!"

"Part it out!"

I meditated on the situation every day. With my smallish garage I couldn't avoid it. The Black Chief was an Exotic—a $25,000 glamour bike, stranded far from home. During its stay, I'd managed to chip its fender on the tail pipe of my vintage. One of Tobin's friends muddied the tank with his sneakers and one of the boys—it was never clear which—bent the ignition key trying to start it up. The truth was the bike was in the way. What's more, I couldn't figure out my feelings for it—what it was to me or how far I was prepared to go to keep it. But instead of riding, I mostly let it sit.

A month passed before an e-mail broke the spell. It was vaguely clandestine, yet to the point: The Black Chief was scheduled for pickup "inside of a weak [sic]."

I was stunned. It was all so low-rent! However faulty my reasoning, I really had expected to keep it awhile—at least until spring.

Within an hour a whiskey-voiced truck dispatcher from Santa Anita called for directions to my house.

I hedged a moment, then grudgingly gave them up.

"Great," she chuckled. "So we know how to get there. Now who the hell's gonna pay for this? You?"

"Wow," I said. "That's a good one! How about the guys that want it back?"

The dispatcher snorted. "Know what? It's hard to get hold of folks when their numbers' disconnected."

Time was tight. I hung up the phone and made for my garage. I swung the door open, propped it with a gas can. For a second I was surprised to see the Black Chief there. Somehow I had already imagined it gone.

October 2003 was as gorgeous as August had been dreadful. For weeks the air stayed warm and fragrant, the skies fair and open, the mountains bathed in sunlight. The month was like a gift, one could think, for hanging in through the fires.

I didn't know where to ride or how long. I knew only that it would be an odd swan song. That in the course of it, I might figure things out. Or not.

In the end, I chose Route 200, the kind of rolling, scenic blacktop winding east along the Blackfoot River for its first fifty miles, then rising steadily into the Rockies. I've ridden my vintage bike on this route several times. Loping along at sixty in the absence of traffic, I always imagined Route 200 was just the kind of road it was built for.

And yet my last vintage ride was a travail: forest fires and construction had made for stop-and-start traffic, and ten miles out my 1947 Chief began to stutter. The farther I rode, the rougher it ran, so by mile 20 I U-turned and limped home, all the way berating myself for whatever bit of maintenance I had once again failed to perform.

The Black Chief started, idled flawlessly. While I sat warming it up, I realized how I'd come to believe there was something heroic in riding vintage, that there was something banal in a new bike. That, without even meaning to, I was now conducting a comparison test: the best of the present versus the worst of the past. Simply put, my vintage is a ride that makes demands. To keep it running and ride it well requires a fierce concentration along with a certain suspension of disbelief. And while it's true my vintage has never broken down on the road, the possibility of it has kept me from taking many long trips.

I flipped down my face screen, rode out in this magic autumn. I ran east with the cool of the Blackfoot River, burst through the shadows of Lubrecht Forest, plunged down towards the Potomac valley plain. A twist of throttle sent me blazing past semis and road-whales, and the Swan range, fifty miles ahead, sprung toward me with each acceleration. I downshifted, banged a left at the giant plastic Hereford colossus marking the Clearwater junction, then shot north up Highway 83, into the Swan River valley. The sun behind me now, my shadow pooled ahead like dark water as I sped along the glacier-pocked ridges I've hunted half my life.

The farther I rode, the less I thought about getting back. What's more, I was beginning to get the whole piano connection: My old bike was ragtime on a barroom piano. This new bike? The "Emperor Concerto" on an ebony concert grand. I knew I couldn't keep it, yet I was falling in love with it anyway, which made us fated, star-crossed. Mostly, I was beginning to think of how wrong I'd been about these bikes. That with the company out of business, maybe, after all, they were real Indians.

The following afternoon, October 21, 2004, a pair of North American Van Line movers arrived, six hours late. They were sheepish, solemn as pallbearers. I was annoyed from waiting and did not conceal it. They parked their seedy-looking van in the alley while I opened my garage, rolled the Black Chief out. The day had grown dreary, and I told them I would leave now, that it would be hard to watch them load. They allowed they understood.

"Are they taking the black bike?" Tobin asked.

"Yeah."

"So where's the piano truck?"

I thought it was a pretty good question, actually.

Half an hour passed before I went out to check on them. The movers had been joined by a third man and they all circled the bike warily.

"Hey man," the oldest one said, clearly embarrassed. "Can you give us a hand with this? None of us ever been on one before..."

When we'd finished loading and they'd buttoned up the truck, I stood in the alley, watched this slipshod outfit pack the Black Chief away to wherever unsuccessful motorcycle revivals finally end up.

There are many good reasons why the second-generation Indians failed: They were too pricey. They were over-marketed, under-produced. There were quality issues and there were too many car guys in the mix. But mostly, the new Indians stayed too derivative for too long.

Still, when I realized what I'd let slip through my fingers, it was tough. Someone had finally built an Indian that would start with a button, cruise at eighty, stop on a dime, and give you an odds-on chance of getting where you wanted to go. Whatever its exact pedigree, the black 2003 PowerPlus Chief was one hell of a ride.

Ford or Chevy, Bud or Miller, Harvard or Yale—fifty years ago, there was Harley or Indian, too. With most things American, you always have that choice, so maybe Indian's indomitable mystique can be best explained as a kind of phantom limb syndrome.

The name alone sold millions of dollars' worth of Canadian sportswear, but fell well short of being the billion-dollar brand name Murray Smith envisioned. Depending on who you talk to, Indian came wrenchingly close to the Rip Van Winkle comeback so many had hoped for, but fell short of that, too.

On a closing note, one deposed executive told me that before he joined Indian in 2001 he did his own "mother-in-law" survey—an informal name-recognition test—to see how many people knew of these bikes.

"Considering Indian hadn't made a machine since the

Korean War, the recognition factor was off the charts," he said. But what impressed him more than that was the odd kind of "oral history" his survey produced.

Like that of the San Diego grandmother, whose family fled the dust bowl in 1934. She recalled how her brother loaded his Indian sidecar with household stuffs "till it looked like a damn pack mule."

Or like that of the Orange County defense attorney who high-fived the photo of his uncle on a flat-track racer whenever he tried a difficult case. Or the Nevada rancher, whose granddad rode an Indian in France during World War I, whose father rode one in Burma in World War II.

"Not only was the recognition there—there were these amazing stories to go with it," the exec shook his head. "Really, what I was getting from these folks was something more akin to religion."

By which he probably meant a uniquely American, motorized kind of Shinto, in which whole twentieth-century family histories were intricately connected with Indian bikes.

I don't know if old motorcycles make a good religion or not. Mostly, I've come to the conclusion that while they might sell a lot of polo shirts and they still might make a great comeback someday, basically Indians are machines to bear stories. That seems to be what they do best. Exactly why this should be is probably for the next generation of cyclists to figure out, and along these lines I have thoughtfully provided my son, Tobin, with more than enough stories to hold his own in this regard: stories of a life caught in the flux between vintage and modernity, and of a father's fateful weakness. Stories of two mythic bikes that once shared his garage, of muddying their tanks with his sneakers. Stories of a night long ago, when a giant semi pulled in out of the smoke. It would seem to bear great pianos, this spectral white Kenworth. But in fact, it would bring something far more exotic. And far more enduring, too.

2007

The Redwood Brigade

Eureka, California, March 17: On a sodden, fog-clotted North Coast morning, a trio of hard-hatted tree-climbers rappelled leisurely down the trunk of a two-hundred foot redwood older than Christianity. Their goal was to evict a slender, spectacled young tree-sitter known as "Remedy."

For team leader Eric Schatz, a Eureka native, it was the shakedown test of America's first professional tree-sitter extraction team.

For Remedy, twenty-six, of Mount Pleasant, Michigan, the eviction would prevent the celebration of her first anniversary aboard the thirteen-feet-in-diameter giant the tree-sitters call "Jerry."

A hundred or so feet below Remedy's four-by-eight foot, tarpaulin-covered redoubt was a mélange of fifteen Humboldt County sheriffs, seven correctional staff, four highway patrolmen, numerous security employees of Pacific Lumber Company (known as PalCo, owners of the tree), various press crews, and a kind of intersectarian mix of environmental activists calling themselves, the "Forest Defenders."

Had they been privy to the conversation above them, they would have heard what, according to both extractor and extractee, was a philosophical debate of near surreal rectitude.

Schatz: "Good morning, Remedy. Hey—while I greatly admire your principals and determination to protect this tree, it's my duty to inform you that this is private property and you're trespassing."

Remedy: "Good morning, Climber Eric. While I appreciate your coming all the way up to apprise me of this, in good conscience I can't abandon this ancient being to PalCo's cavalier and non-sustainable harvest policies."

Or something like that.

After a couple hour's discussion, Remedy at last slipped her hands into her "lock box" (a homemade manacle chained around Jerry's trunk) and proceeded to take herself hostage.

The extraction team then hauled a fifty-pound compressed-air powered grinder up on a rope. As the grinder ground and Remedy's manacles heated up, Schatz stood by, cooled her arms with Perrier. Hours later, the manacle severed, the climbers handcuffed Remedy with plastic ties, strapped her into an evacuation harness. Schatz lifted her in his arms and the two were lowered gently to the ground on half-inch, sixteen-strand braided nylon rope. According to at least one witness, they cut a dashing figure.

To PalCo's way of thinking, this engagement was probably a smashing success—just the type of orderly, pro forma extraction (or "rescue," as PalCO describes them) the embattled company had hoped for.

On the other hand, the Forest Defenders were bummed. By the time Remedy and Wren, another sitter, were brought down and packed in a sheriff's car, the activists attempted to block the road, and a baton-and-pepper-spray fracas erupted. It lasted ten minutes, resulted in several arrests.

When I spoke with Remedy a few days later, her anniversary spoiled, she reported glumly that she was treated well enough "up there."

"So they weren't goons or anything, the PalCo guys?"

"No, they were very smooth. And Eric—well, he'll charm the pants right off you."

"Does that mean he was gentlemanly?"

"Oh, extremely so. Outwardly. But inwardly? Inwardly, he's sick."

Freshwater, a steep, heavily-logged drainage about three miles north of Eureka, has for nearly a decade been an epicenter in the fight to save Humboldt County's remaining old growth trees. The acreage, thanks to the Greenwood Heights Road, is easily accessible to loggers, activists, and media alike, resulting in an on-going melodrama in which both trees and sitters have taken starring roles. (For the most part in this production, PalCo has played the villain.)

At first just an annoyance, the un-harvested redwoods the sitters occupy has become an increasing source of frustration to the financially strapped company. Until recently, they could do little about it. Then, in early March, the company got a restraining order from a federal judge allowing them to physically remove the sitters.

This was far easier said than done.

That's when they turned to Schatz, a local arborist.

One of maybe a dozen old growth specialists in the country, Schatz climbs these giants routinely to prune away deadwood or storm damage. Or he may rig and remove tons of rotted treetop hanging over a million dollar home. All these operations he will perform without ruffling a shingle, harming the tree, or fracturing his skull.

Schatz's been doing this for thirty-one years, a span of time over which he estimates he's climbed one hundred thousand vertical feet, or well beyond the stratosphere. Part of his skill as a big tree climber is to take something that appears insanely hazardous, make it seem a perfectly reasonable, even quotidian thing to do.

It isn't.

Professionals at Schatz's level have long understood that macho has no place in their world. Their survival depends on cool, not daring; caution, not swagger. These were exactly the intangibles he looked for when he first formed his team.

To qualify, team members needed a minimum of ten years' old growth experience, plus extensive training in alpine rescue, non-violent problem solving, and crowd psychology. For starters.

On a rainy Friday night, I met Schatz and an E-team climber called Ox at a Eureka coffee shop. They were cordial but extremely wary. They told me, point blank, they didn't trust the press. To make matters worse, an activist called "Tree" threw himself under Schatz's Suburban on his way over to meet with me. Schatz barely avoided running him over.

I stirred my coffee. "Are you guys still rattled?"

The two exchanged glances. Schatz is wiry, compact, a

youthful forty-six year old with a Guardsman's mustache. Ox is tall and powerfully built, a soft spoken, fifty-year-old grandfather.

"More and more," Ox reflected, "'rattled' is a way of life around here."

Here's how Schatz's operation works:

The E-team (as they call themselves) totals six climbers, which they try to work three to a tree. Their ground support group—belayers, suppliers and such—might include another half dozen, plus whatever law enforcement seems appropriate.

In theory, the team will stay operational until the situation is resolved. They do not rely heavily on stealth. Because of sophisticated activist technology (cell phones, computers, walkie-talkies), the size of the entourage, and because rigging a big tree ascent takes time, the element of surprise is pretty much eliminated.

"Hell," Schatz told me. "They not only know exactly when we're coming, they know us all by name!"

At the occupied tree, the E-Team uses a crossbow to shoot a monofilament line through a crotch one hundred feet up. With this, they haul up a climbing rope, rig it for single line ascent, then one by one, head up into the canopy.

"Every tree's different," says Schatz. "We try to avoid coming up under the sitter's platforms, but lots of times we can't. And when that happens, well, that's always dicey. They say they're nonviolent, but...let's just say, some take the idea more seriously than others."

In truth, never is the E-team more vulnerable than at this point, and their safe ascent depends entirely on a kind of gentlemen's agreement with the sitters that all encounters will be nonviolent.

Seeking the high ground, E-teamers climb to a point

well above the activists. They pick a staging area, belay themselves, and set their evacuation rigging—usually a pair of three-hundred-foot descent lines run through alloy pulleys and anchored to a belaying device.

Then, like an aerial boarding party, the team rappels to the sitter's bivouac below where the first order of business is a kind of on-the-spot evaluation: Does the sitter pose a physical threat? Is the sitter hypothermic? Stoned? Malnourished? Rational?

While Schatz and Ox talked easily about procedure, technique, and equipment, and while they were justifiably proud of their safety record to date, they talked less easily about the activists and their modus operandi. These were described in tense, sobering dispatches: marginal clothing, low-protein diets in cold, wet weather. Limited climbing skills, lots of dope, and most ominously, lots of makeshift safety gear. Since 1998, two sitters have died from questionable belays, another was severely injured.

But most troubling to the team is that they never know how a sitter will react to their presence—that is, how far he or she might go to make a stand.

One young woman stripped naked when the team arrived. They waited till the cold weather forced her to dress.

Schatz recounts, unprintably, the time another sitter doused him with a water bucket.

Things, in the E-team's view, keep escalating. A few days after my visit, Schatz called to tell me a contingent from Earth Liberation Front made an impromptu visit to his home where they informed Schatz, cryptically, that whatever he did to the tree sitters, they were prepared to do to him.

Then there was "Phoenix," who slipped past security, made his way into the outer branches of one tree, and free climbed over one hundred feet straight up right past the E-Team, already landed on the sitter's platform.

"He was headed for our belays when I tackled him," said Schatz. "Ox and I wrestled him down and sat on him, at which point the kid went mental. He said he was suicidal. He shook us off, made a dive for the edge of the platform, got halfway off before we could grab his legs and stop him. You can't tell me that guy wasn't smoking *some*thing—the way he fought us? And that was after climbing a hundred feet straight up!"

In the course of our conversation, I avoided asking Schatz and Ox any kind of Big Question. In truth, I was far less interested in their views on old growth harvest than I was in the climbing/rescue skills that allow the safe extraction of an unwilling tree sitter from a two-hundred-foot tree. Still, by evening's end, the two remained sober and wary. As if the interview was a kind of sucker punch waiting to happen.

Before I left Eureka, I was invited by Remedy and the Forest Defenders to view the video they'd made of a March 19 E-Team operation. I was received hospitably by them at their Freshwater digs, where I sprawled on the living room floor to watch it amid a welter of dogs, teamugs, and amped-up activists.

Leaving aside all the oft-expressed, fervently-held opinions of both sides in this consuming and fulminatory environmental debate, if you chose to view Remedy's extraction as a model of big tree decorum (as I did), the operation revealed by the Forest Defender's footage was significantly messier, vastly more frightening.

A new sitter, "Mystique," re-occupied Remedy's old tree, and the footage opened with her one hundred feet above the old bivouac, bear-hugging the tree's ten-inch diameter top, apparently un-belayed.

We then cut to Schatz, working his way up from below. Depending on who you listen to, he has either provoked a game of Redwood chicken, or Mystique has blundered into a jam of her own making and Schatz is performing a rescue.

Though the crowd below is raucous—hazing Schatz, shouting encouragement to Mystique—the canopy drama is unmiked, silent. The video is overexposed, so the climbers are in silhouette, like puppets in Balinesian shadow play.

Schatz draws close to Mystique's perch and stops.

The two seem to talk.

Then the crowd goes silent. Mystique, fresh out of vertical, veers abruptly to the horizontal, edges her way out a branch the diameter of a baseball. She shuffles a couple feet then freezes.

Schatz speaks to her. Whatever he says, it has the wrong effect, and he watches helplessly while Mystique, in the name of protection, tosses an anemic, prusik cord over a remarkably unsubstantial looking sucker, hangs onto it like a subway strap while she edges straight for the void. A bad move in any tree, and at two-hundred feet, it's the worst you can make.

Schatz climbs level with Mystique, belays himself with his lanyard. They talk briefly.

Something gives way and Mystique pitches forward, grabs a handful of redwood twigs to stop her fall.

Now the crowd comes alive. They badmouth Schatz, tell Mystique they love her, that the trees love her, too. "Be strong," they tell her, "be strong!" There's swearing, weeping, imprecations. Someone calls 911. Except for some random ululation, it sounds quite a bit like Saturday Night Wrestling. Yet the pair up the tree is breathtaking;

like spirits cast in shadow. Anything can happen now.

Two hundred feet above the forest floor with no place left to go, their conversation looks feverish, strangely intimate.

According to Schatz, it went like this:

"Listen to me. We're in a bad spot. You go out further, it's pure suicide. You're a tough cookie, an awesome climber, and now everyone knows it. You've got nothing left to prove."

According to Mystique, it was like this:

"Hey. You fall out of this tree now, neither me or my crew's responsible. We'll testify it was suicide, plain and simple."

Oddly enough, both parties agree on what happens next:

Schatz doffs his safety glasses. He's crying.

"Listen," he says "I'm really afraid right now. I don't want to die today and I don't want you to die, either. Please. Help me get us out of this mess."

Mystique, crying too, agrees, allows Schatz to loop a lanyard around her and gently pull her in.

Back on earth, the arboreal rapprochement disappears like vapor: Mystique claims she was struck in the mouth by a carabineer during her evacuation; that a petulant E-Team lowered her to the ground "by my chest."

Before I packed to leave, I spoke to Andrew Edwards, reporter for the *North Coast Journal*, a local weekly. He was convinced that the climbers and sitters had a pretty good rapport. He said he'd seen them joke around, try to recruit each other, share Powerade and climbing lore.

In the trees, things seemed to work, he said. "It's the crowd on the ground that's weird…that's where things go sour."

It reminded me of something Remedy said when I asked her what it was like back on terra firma after a year in the tree. She shook her head, smiled vaguely. "It's amazing how good it smells up there," she said. "And how much the ground stinks."

2007

Jesus Just Got Evel

Evel Knievel was a great American hell-raiser. He grew up in a hard-nosed mining town, jumped tailings piles on his Schwinn, learned quickly that his strong suit was his guts. From 1965 to 1981, he made three hundred motorcycle jumps of ever-increasing distance and audacity. Starting with a pen full of rattlers for a failing Harley dealership in Idaho, in a couple years he was stunt-jumping nationwide: cars, Mack trucks, double-decker buses, the Caesar's Palace fountains, and most famously, the Snake River Canyon, a jump spoiled by a premature parachute. In the course of these years, he suffered numerous concussions, broke thirty different bones, spent half his time in the hospital. He made millions of dollars, partied with the stars, flew around in a Lear jet, drove his kids to the fishing hole in a yellow Ferrari V-12. His style came from various sixties icons: the white-caped outfits from Elvis Presley, the motor mouth from Muhammad

Ali, the rockabilly hair from Jerry Lee Lewis. But put him on a Harley-Davidson Sportster and he rode like nobody else in the world. He also crashed like nobody else.

When he died of pulmonary fibrosis on November 30, 2007, his family announced they would "throw" a funeral, and that the event would "bear Evel's signature," which could mean just about anything, knowing Knievel. The funeral would take place in his hometown of Butte, Montana, a gritty, hard-partying mountain town whose St. Patrick's Day revels draw crowds in the tens of thousands. Factor in this proclivity with Knievel's many stuntman pals and enough black leather to start a shoe factory, and Butte officials anticipated a send-off of near unprecedented fervor. But if you were looking for someone to pop a screaming, block-long wheelie out of the parking lot and lead Knievel to the sweet hereafter, well, you'd come to the wrong place.

Monday morning, December 10, was cold and blustery. We got a late start driving down from Helena, but managed to park just a block from the Civic Center. Five minutes before the event, we strolled easily past a fleet of phantom-gray stretch Cadillacs, an NBC satellite link, and a squad of extremely husky ushers in snow white XXL mourning suits. Moving briskly to the sign-in desk, we took a program, went inside, were able to find a seat immediately.

At the south end of the hall, beneath a bank of red poinsettias, Evel Knievel lay in state. His coffin was rustic pine and he wore his signature white racing leathers, which featured a red, white, and blue chevron down the front. To one side of the coffin sat a snow white pickup, a matching chevron across its hood. To the other side was a photo gallery of his most spectacular jumps. Above the funeral bier a huge slide projector marched through photos of his life, accompanied by a soundtrack of country songs.

Because of this year's extended elk hunting season, there was plenty of camouflage in the crowd. Lots of Carhartt work jackets, lots of black leather, of course, and a significant number of people who walked with limps. There were a surprising number of toddlers, most of them not at all into it. The media had projected overflow crowds in the thousands, but at five past eleven, as "My Way" played for a second time, the 7,500-seat Butte Civic Center was half empty.

Special guests included actor Matthew McConaughey, narrator of the History Channel's Knievel biography; ABC Sports producer Doug Wilson; the Crystal Cathedral's Reverend Robert Schuller, who'd baptized Knievel last April; professional stuntman Gene Sullivan, of the Jump for Jesus Motorcycle Club; former heavyweight champion Smokin' Joe Frazier; and former Montana governor Judy Martz, who'd grown up with Knievel. When Martz spoke, she blamed the empty seats on the weather, explaining it was too cold for the Harley crowd to ride. But bikers can also drive cars, and besides, it wasn't really that cold, and so some of us got the uneasy feeling the absentees knew something we didn't. The rumors of an admission charge had proved false. On the other hand, the event soon began to resemble a bait and switch; it promised to be a tribute but ended up more a revival, with the Lamb of God methodically thrashing another wild Dionysian heart.

Certainly the funeral delivered its moments of fancy. The first of these came when Reverend Schuller introduced Martz as "Montana's twice-elected governor." Martz was, most emphatically, one term, but she did not bother to correct him. She moved quickly past the subject of how Knievel became who he was, went on to describe his eleventh-hour epiphany at length, ended with the statement, "He is probably now worshipping with the Saints."

For some of us the task of picturing Matthew, Mark, Luke, and Evel was too tall an order. It was easier to imagine him jumping the Berkeley Pit, a massive Superfund site up the mountain that's reported to be wider than the River Styx. Mostly, though, this inflationist oratory set the tone for the rest of the funeral, which consisted largely of triumphant accounts of his conversion. Indeed, from these accounts, and in a hunting community like Butte, it wasn't far-fetched to think of Knievel's soul as a certified Boone and Crockett, the kind of trophy soul only Hunter Thompson's might outscore.

Knievel's friend and producer, Doug Wilson, provided some relief with his assertion that Knievel "was actually not a very good motorcycle rider. Are you kidding? All those crashes? On the other hand, he was an absolutely world-class showman." Wilson went on to relate Knievel's response when a woman from the BBC asked if his failure to jump the Snake River Canyon had damaged his credibility. Knievel turned to her and replied, "No canyon or woman I jumped ever damaged my credibility."

The only one to bring it all home was Evel's son, Robbie Knievel. A daring stuntman after his father's heart, Robbie embarked first on a puzzling, extremely high-risk monologue on the art of "duck-plucking," finally righted himself, and came roaring back to declaim, "I am the son of the Greatest Daredevil in the World!"

Almost before the words were out, the crowd whooped, shouted, and cheered, and for the first and only time that day, the Butte Civic Center came alive. There it was in spades: the bona fide, bare-naked Knievel bravado, that thing the beleaguered audience came to hear.

Beyond argument, the grieving process is very personal, and each of us is entitled to find comfort the best way we can. But the dying Knievel was so frail, all the star-powered salvation rhetoric so relentless that in the end the saving of his soul seemed more like a corporate takeover than an act of grace. Along these lines, it seemed reasonable to ask, if Knievel's salvation was such a rock solid slam-dunk kind of deal, then why were so many people selling it so hard?

Reverend Schuller provided the closing remarks. With the best tan in the house, he spoke at length on the integrity of Evel's conversion, as if we might be harboring doubts. It was unfortunate that it took place on April Fool's Day, but Schuller is an extraordinary speaker, with a voice that could soar from a gravelly whisper all the way to a cosmic thunderclap.

"The eyes have it! The eyes do not lie!" Schuller kept insisting. He certainly gave it his all. Indeed, if he'd had a tachometer, he would have revved it out right to the redline. Yet in the end, the harder he worked it, the more people stood up and filed out, satisfied, apparently, that there was nothing more left to see.

We went directly to a bar. We ended up at the M&M, a Butte landmark that up until a 2005 remodel had not closed its doors for a hundred years.

"Couldn't believe my eyes," said the bartender, shaking his head. "This was supposed to be the biggest deal ever, but the Met Bar (across the street from the Civic Center) was almost dead, and that was always Evel's favorite."

We ordered a round of beers, and some of us had whiskey. All of us, as it happened, were over fifty, and in light of this fact and the gravity of the occasion, we began to talk earnestly about the aging process. In particular we talked about the question of memory—what was memorable, and what was not. Eventually we came to grips with the fact we'd driven seventy miles to the funeral of the most outrageous guy to live in these parts, and it wasn't very memorable at all. Were we within our rights to complain, or was this simply bad form on our part?

We ended up watching the big-screen TV above us, which featured, of all things, live CNN coverage of Evel Knievel, lying in state.

"Talk about your relativism," somebody said.

We looked all around the mostly empty bar, sipped our beers the way you do when it looks like you'll end up partying by yourself. Where was everyone? we wondered.

2007

Auguring the Great Divide

"I'll give it to you straight," Marilyn said, bearding me by my aging Kenmore. "Your place is cute, fairly pulled together. Great location, terrific curb appeal. Unfortunately, there's plenty of homes like this in the U District now. And in terms of the market, if it hasn't quite flat lined, you could say the party's almost over."

"Well," I said. "That doesn't sound promising."

It was a Tuesday, the Realtor Open House day. Marilyn arrived toward the end of this event, lingered till everyone left, then caught me in the basement, where with its bare pipes, half-assed wiring, and cat-box miasma, I tended to feel most vulnerable.

One of several total strangers who held my future in their hands, she gave me a look beyond compassion, a look that seemed to say she wanted to be kind, but that she understood when kindness wouldn't do.

"Fred," she said. "May I call you Fred, by the way?"

"Sure," I said. "I guess."

"Fred, we live in very dicey times. The world is getting hotter, the icepack's melting, the North Koreans have nukes now, the Iranians do too, and that's not to mention the mess over in Iraq..."

She paused; a drain pipe gurgled cheerfully overhead, my 1952 Crosley upright freezer switched on with a noise like a coffee mill full of rocks. There was a dreadful, diagnostic intimacy to the moment that both fascinated and repelled me.

"This isn't what you want to hear," she said.

"You're right about that." I told her.

"But here's the deal, Fred. You might be sitting on your little house a while before it dawns on you to drop your price, but that's entirely up to you. Personally, I find the market doesn't loosen up till the week after Super Bowl Sunday. Meanwhile, I'd say do yourself a favor and read a book by Jared Diamond called *Collapse*. In times like these, it's an eye-opener, and it will certainly give you scale."

I followed her to the door, watched her pull away in her Chevy Suburban. You couldn't get a broader market analysis than the one I'd just had, not even if the Cumaean Sibyl was your agent. As luck would have it, I happened to be reading *Collapse*. I wondered how she could possibly have known this, and if Marilyn's point was that the current decline in university housing prices was a natural outgrowth of the degradation of the Polynesian and Anasazi civilizations. The way things were going, you couldn't really rule that out. In any case, I had to go lie down.

Once you start thinking about omens, signs, and such, they become almost impossible to ignore. Along these lines our move had some lulus: the seedy-looking crows who came to hang out in our yard, the rising flatulence of our dog with the appearance of each new suitcase, the unexplained demise of our microwave, halfway through a bag of Redenbacher's. There was the cliff-hanger senatorial contest that threatened to raise then dash our hopes, and of course, my mounting apprehension with moving across the Great Divide, a term which, once you're past fifty, fairly begs for metaphorical status. And the signs kept on coming, too; they were stuck to this move just like cat hair to a wad of Juicy Fruit, which, speaking of signs, is what I happened to be scraping off my floor the day Marilyn dropped by.

Moving stinks. First you're dealing with that keep-it-or-pitch-it mind-set, then the wanton existentialism of packing your life up in liquor boxes. But the moving process pales beside the actual selling of your house, and in this case I'd spent twenty pretty good years in this place. It's where I got married, wrote books, buried friends, birthed babies, got drunk, got sober, and restored two wonderfully slutty old motorcycles. Suddenly the mere pule of a cell phone sent me into a frenzy of sweeping, dusting, and low-rent cover-up repairs; sent me spritzing around the house with a jug of 409 and a rag, as if I'd rub away any trace I'd ever lived there. The move was starting to get to me, let's face it.

Back to the Great Divide thing: The first time I crossed it was thirty years ago, when I left the East Coast for good. I fell in love with the West, with the people, with the idea that the ten thousand-foot up-thrust that separated the first and second acts of my life was as remote and inaccessible as the Khyber Pass. For this reason, any move eastward—even the hundred-odd miles to Helena—was more or less equivalent to moving back home with my mom. Loutish crows, divinizing realtors, and the like—all fueled a mounting geo-phobia, made the move seem dark, maybe ill-starred, who could say? In any event it might have run away with me, had it not been for the events of October 4, 2006.

I was in the alley, recycling aluminum cans, when I heard Mick Jagger speak, plain as day.

"Testing?" he said. "Two, three?"

The voice was unmistakable, the clarity was remarkable. It seemed like it was coming right out of a Friskies mixed-grill can, until I realized what was happening— mere blocks away at Grizzly Stadium, the Rolling Stones were checking sound for the greatest show to hit these parts since Houdini played the Wilma.

I stood there, poised to hear what might come next, but it seemed like the sound check was over, and anyway I had to go wipe the cocoa stains from the kitchen cabinets. But here's the thing: Considering Jagger's hallmark cats-and-crows shtick, this event would seem a natural for my collection of weird signs. But something totally different happened. I know Mick and I are the same age, know that Mick's hard-wired just to boogie till he pukes. The idea that I'd shrink from a hundred-mile move seemed not just unacceptable—it was embarrassing. I decided then and there I didn't get out enough.

That night the skies above Grizzly Stadium were lit with techno-borealis. My children soon discovered that in spite of many precautions the Stones' production crew had taken, by standing on our picnic table you could hear the band loud and clear, and I taught them to do the Mashed Potatoes while Mick sang "Tumblin' Dice."

A few weeks later, regardless of what the signs might say, winter was bearing down and everyone understood what that meant: it was time to bust a move across the pass.

We've been on the east slope six months now. The ice cap's still melting, the Anasazis are still long gone. On the other hand, our dog stopped farting, the Democrats won a squeaker, and we sold our house a month after we arrived here. True, we dropped our price some, but we did close before Super Bowl Sunday. And more important, before our monster second mortgage came due. I've since learned Helena's not quite as far east as the Adirondacks, and that it reminds me of the best parts of Missoula, except with better weather. There may be a spate of omens happening here, too, but I'm still too busy moving to notice. Meanwhile, the new house is bright and spacious, filled with clear, east-slope light, waiting for another twenty years of adventures—who knows? Thanks, Mick. I needed that!

Slime and Transfiguration

At forty-thousand feet it might look like an alpine lake. A little closer to the ground, and things look different. On its best day, Lake Berkeley looks more like an impact crater on the back side of Uranus. The steep walls that encircle it are a chthonic, sulfurous hue. Its waters are implacable, calm and dark. There is little sign of life.

Of course, looks aren't everything. Lake Berkeley is also a kind of Mojito of heavy metals, and it's rising steadily, posing catastrophic threats to the local aquifer and to ecosystems hundreds of miles away. It is so toxic that in 1995 it burned the gizzards right out of a flight of unsuspecting snow geese who had the bad luck to use it for a stopover. The event will long be remembered as an Ecological Day of Infamy, but really, the fact this lake exists at all makes it a monument to the towering indifference of the mining industry.

By now everyone knows the story of how Lake Berkeley came to be—the way the most lucrative economy Montana's ever seen devoured itself and died; the way the once bustling city of Butte morphed from the Richest Hill on Earth to the Biggest Superfund Site; the way that on April 22, 1982, as a kind of Earth Day surprise, Arco stopped the pumps that drained the pit and went back to wherever they came from, leaving the population of Butte (down 60 percent from the heydays of the 1920s) to meditate on the thirty billion gallons of toxic bullion steeping away in a mile-wide, thousand-foot-deep lake, right there in the heart of the city. Mostly though, it left them to come to grips with the fact that, while the lake grows more ominous each day, beyond a controversial strategy to treat the lake with lime—as if it were a giant outhouse—nobody really knows what happens next.

Strangely, about the same time the lake's notoriety couldn't get much worse, something truly miraculous happened: in the summer of 1995, somebody discovered life in Lake Berkeley.

"Slime?" everyone said. "There's slime in the Berkeley Pit?"

Of course, there's nothing very remarkable about *Euglena mutabilis*. It's your basic lime green pond scum. But when the pond in question has a pH somewhere between battery acid and a rancid Mountain Dew, when the pond is spiked with arsenic, lead, and cadmium—well, it's either something very special, or else it's something very weird. Indeed, for the twelve years the lake had been forming, scientists were so focused on its extraordinary composition that it never really occurred to anyone such a habitat might support life.

Enter Andrea Stierle, professor of biochemistry at Butte's Montana Tech. No less astounded than the next person, she quickly got past her surprise and with her husband, organic chemist Don Stierle, went to work taking water samples, eventually isolating, then culturing the nearly fifty odds-defying organisms they were amazed to find living there. Some were fungal, some bacterial. Most of them just survived there, yet a few of them were thriving, possibly from the lack of competition. These species—the overachievers—the Stierles decided to call "extremophiles." Here was the place they'd start.

The Stierles, veteran prospectors for medical curatives, knew immediately they were on to something. In such a hostile environment, the microbes they discovered needed to have an extremely active enzyme-inhibiting capacity, which could eventually translate into a potent natural curative. All bacteria and fungi produce substances that are poisonous to invasive species, and these substances, known as "secondary metabolites," present the richest, and least explored, frontier for potential medicinal compounds.

Andrea and her husband, Don, are that rarity of rarities, a married couple and research partners. The Stierles, who've been together nearly thirty years, met at San Diego State, where Don received his degree in organic chemistry. In 1980 Don took what was to have been a nine-month position at Butte's Montana Tech. While there, Andrea began work on a doctorate degree at Montana State, in Bozeman. They soon grew to love Montana, forgot why it was they needed to leave. In the late 1980s the two teamed up to research exotic compounds, first in the field of agriculture (they discovered an agent used in knapweed control in the sponge populations off Bermuda). They soon realized there was little funding available in agriculture, so they tried their hand with natural curatives, which Andrea describes as "truly, the world's oldest profession."

The decision led them on a quest for medicinals in the Northwest, where in the early 1990s they came across a compound known as taxol in the bark of the Pacific yew tree. Taxol turned out to be an effective anti-cancer drug, but the trees were in limited supply. At this point the couple implemented a process they describe as "biorational serendipity," a method combining scientific deduction with old-fashioned bulldog detective work. By this means they eventually discovered that the taxol present in yew bark was produced not by the yew itself, but by a discreet, and previously unknown, fungus that had taken up residence there.

Using their biorationally serendipitous approach to Lake Berkeley (which they're coming to view as a giant Petri dish), the Stierles have so far identified compounds that show promise for the treatment of migraines, cancer, and even depression. But most serendipitous of all is the discovery that the alga *Chlorella vulgaris* appears to actually "eat" heavy metals, while other algae have been observed to reduce acidity. If this is really the case, and if these algae can be heavily cultured, the impact down the road would be profound. What are the odds that the very place that nearly drowned in its own poisons would generate the source of its redemption?

Billionaires Without Boundaries

Somewhere on his 9,500-acre ranch in Montana's Paradise Valley, maybe as he watched the sun-dazzled Yellowstone River slide by the 12,000-foot Absaroka Mountains, Wall Street tycoon and self-described conservationist Wade Dokken must have had a vision: he would create a new kind of luxury community in the heart of the American West. Different from the typical recreation-based developments, utopian in concept, his Ameya Preserve would be a place of unsurpassed beauty, where bright and uncommonly well-heeled people could, however briefly, take their ease in a community implementing the kind of cutting-edge technology that could one day save the planet. Along these lines, Ameya (Sanskrit for "without boundaries") would be powered entirely by solar, wind, or geothermal sources, the buildings constructed according to the most advanced environmental specifications. Most prominently, Ameya would also be designed to "zero out," which means that the carbon emitted in the construction process would be scrupulously calculated, then offset by planting forest tracts elsewhere in the West.

In place of golf or skiing, residents could participate in a variety of Chautauqua-like events conducted by Ameya "cultural directors," community members with distinguished backgrounds in the arts and sciences. Indeed, the people Ameya would have on board include some of the brightest stars on the American scene: best-selling author and restaurateur Alice Waters; soprano Renée Fleming; paleontologist Jack Horner; and former head of New York's Metropolitan Museum, Thomas Hoving, to name a few.

In terms of the best and brightest, Dokken could hardly hope for better. The only thing he might wish is that Park County locals stay too dazzled to notice that his project is a meticulously designed biosphere for the über-rich, built smack in the middle of habitat that conservationists are fighting to save.

It's fair to say that for the world's wealthiest, environmental issues have not always been a prime concern. Often enough, this is exactly how they got rich, and nowhere is this more true than in the American West, where the ravening extractive industries have run roughshod for over a century. It's not surprising that plush developments like Big Sky's Yellowstone Club (where skiers of serious means schuss trademarked "Private Powder") occasionally have issues with the EPA.

The ultimate glitzification of sleepy mountain towns like Aspen and Jackson was more about insouciance than noblesse oblige. So to many it was refreshing to hear a high-end developer talking knowledgably about aquifers and habitat depletion. At first Dokken got a lot of good ink about how painstakingly the initial proposal was put together. "I was kind of blown away [with it]," said Jim Barrett, director of the Park County Environmental Council in Livingston. "It's not perfect, but if we were to write the handbook on smart growth development... that's basically what it was."

A North Dakota native, Dokken made his fortune on Wall Street as president of American Skandia, a financial services company. He sold Skandia to Prudential in 2003, returned west to deal in high-end real estate. A tycoon who votes Democratic, a developer who sees himself as a conservationist, Dokken had straddled enough fences to know that if he was to build Ameya in a place like Paradise Valley, it would help to win over the community, which was a fairly sophisticated one, at that.

For years the cowboys, ranchers, artists, and working people of Livingston coexisted peaceably with celebrities, from movie folk like Sam Peckinpah and Jeff Bridges to famous writers like Jim Harrison and Tim Cahill. What they all had in common was they knew a great place when they saw one, and they liked it the way it was. In this manner, except for bank account, notoriety, and charisma, their move to the Montana Rockies was much like my own. I know a good place when I see one, too.

By last June, 2007, Ameya seeded the local papers with ads trumpeting the smorgasbord of benefits the development, were it approved, could bring to Park County. These included a large spike in property tax revenues, a $50,000 donation to the rural fire department, the building of one Habitat for Humanity house for every fifty homes built at Ameya, funding for two advanced-placement teachers at Park County High School, and a 200-acre reservation for Livingston's "Farms for Families," a local program that promotes organic farming.

If such high-flying PR made locals a bit leery ("One can't help but notice the lengths to which Ameya is going...to make their project palatable to the public," one letter to the *Livingston Enterprise* observed), the discovery that Ameya would try to buy two sections of adjoining public land made them downright skeptical. Though the project was still in the early stages, by July locals began airing their doubts in a series of blogs and letters to the papers.

While some thought it laudable that Ameya eschewed the traditional 6,000-square-foot "Log-Mahal" for more discreet 4,000-footers, and that these homes would be powered renewably, and that the acreage upon which they'd be built was subjected to exhaustive impact studies, many struggled with pronouncements like "Ameya will be the most sustainable community ever built." Other project descriptions seemed almost nonsensical. A "private national park?" A "gated community with a conscience?" What in the world could that mean? Finally, Ameya's assertion that "this project preserves natural resources that couldn't be preserved by any other means" involved the kind of death-defying, leap-of-faith logic few besides Dokken could manage.

Neither did it help that Ameya had a way of getting ahead of itself, and was prone to make claims it couldn't substantiate; for example, it was news to Thomas Hoving to learn he'd accepted Ameya's invitation, and it was news to the Corporation for the Northern Rockies to read that they'd already endorsed Dokken's project. More to the point, locals objected to a large-scale development built in a fire-prone drainage, they objected to the fact these were second, third, or even fourth vacation homes, and they objected to what seemed to be Dokken's selective environmentalism.

Park County wildlife ecologist Peter Feigley, who smelled green wash early on, questioned Ameya's principles on a popular blog called Luxist. "How many homes do the prospective clients [already] own, and how large are they? Think of how much jet fuel and gasoline is wasted by the ultra wealthy and their families, bopping around between their various homes and resorts." Feigley eventually described Ameya as "a sham; targeting wealthy and naïve, if not arrogant, individuals."

For Dokken, this proved too much. When you cracked on the ultra wealthy, you were cracking on his people, and he couldn't let such a remark go unchallenged. He fired off a letter to Park County planner Mike Inman in which, among other things, he berated his critics for "class envy," claiming remarks like Feigley's were directed "at people who have had more success in life than the letter writers and blog writers...Perhaps they were smarter. Perhaps they worked harder. Perhaps they managed their money better..."

There followed a brief communal gasp. Had the locals just been scolded for not respecting their betters? Had Dokken been drinking? Whatever the case, everyone knew what really happened: A millionaire finally used the C-word.

It's weird to be discussing "class" in the twenty-first-century West. For openers, many of us moved here precisely to get away from such a concept, and besides, the West is known for its frontier egalitarianism and hard-nosed reality checks—a beautiful but uncompromising place you were required to meet on its own terms. In short, it was a place where old-world conceits like "class" and "privilege" would get you nowhere, quickly.

Still, the fact the high-end real estate market fairly suppurates with descriptors like "elite," "privileged," and "exclusive" underscores an unpleasant truth: the people who can afford to buy up the most beautiful spots in the West have no intention of leaving their core values back home. This would also seem to underscore Dokken's contention that the development of areas like the Paradise Valley is inevitable, and if he doesn't do it, some less visionary person will.

Be that as it may, Dokken seems to want it all; he wants to make money doing something that seems, environmentally speaking, indefensible, but he wants to be well thought of, too. Following his now infamous letter to the Park County Planning Board, he quickly wrote the *Enterprise* that he "deeply regretted [his] choice of words." He went on to state that "a careful reading of the remainder of the letter...revealed an outline of environmental initiatives..." that would, essentially, authenticate his commitment to conservation.

Mostly, however, a careful reading of the letter brings forth a number of statements that seem in direct opposition to the term as most people understand it. Consider: "Ameya Preserve will be the first carbon neutral community in the U.S....addressing the potentially greatest issue of our day in the single most responsible manner." On any green scale, how is the clearing, excavation, and paving of elk habitat to build baronial-size, seldom-used luxury homes to be viewed as "responsible," no matter how they are powered, or how many organic farming projects, easements, or carbon switcheroos are in the works?

In any event Dokken was hard pressed to put the genie back in the bottle. For weeks the *Enterprise* printed responses like the following:

"It is difficult to forgive Mr. Dokken for insinuating... that we are stupid enough not to recognize a land speculator when we see one."

"The stark reality is that the Ameya Preserve will turn...Paradise Valley into upscale suburbia."

"One piece of advice for you, Mr. Dokken. Don't get stuck in a snowdrift coming out of your 'preserve'...you may find that nobody wants to stop and help you."

And finally: "Years from now, we will look back on the loss of these public sections with regret. The developer and his clients are the only ones who will be happy."

The coming summer, 2008, promises interesting times for Ameya. While many elite developments have been hit hard by the slumping market (Idaho's Promontory and Montana's Yellowstone Club are among them), Ameya spokesmen claim interest in the lots is unabated, and in spite of local opinion the development goes apace. Along these lines, it's worth noting that in the past month he sold 4,000 acres of Ameya land to neighbor and fellow billionaire, candy magnate Giorgio Perfetti. The deal helped eliminate most of Dokken's debt, and helped move his project along toward final approval. Interestingly enough, Perfetti wanted to buy the land because he didn't want to watch it get developed.

The real genius to Ameya Preserve is that it foresees that global warming might take the fun out of being rich—what if they wouldn't let you jet to two vacation homes per week? But at Ameya the wealthiest people in the world would get to feel that, with no noticeable change in their habits or behavior, they could still be part of the solution. In this way what Dokken offers most closely resembles the medieval sale of Indulgences; instead of examining or changing behavior, well-heeled sinners simply paid the fine, went right on sinning. After all, they could afford it.

2010

The Demon Beetles
of Thunder Drive

In the palm of your hand, they don't look like much: a black bug the size of a chocolate sprinkle. Put one under a microscope and the mountain pine beetle, *Dendroctonus ponderosae*, is hairy and lethal-looking, a shovel-faced, tank-like chewing machine with legs. Since the first outbreaks began, in the early 1990s, the beetles have infested more than 81,700 square miles of North American forests, an area larger than Nebraska. Last year, 2009, in my home state of Montana alone, the plague more than doubled—from 1.2 million acres in 2008 to 2.7 million in 2009. Depending on whom you talk to, this makes *D. ponderosae* either the most destructive insect in the recorded history of North American forests or, as some ecologists see it, a massive influx of "ecosystem engineers" working tirelessly to improve woodland biodiversity. Call me anthropocentric, but the idea of a bug in the driver's seat doesn't inspire much confidence.

Take this lodgepole I'm standing next to, one of the beetle's favorite pines. It is green-needled and vigorous looking, but it's actually dead as a phone pole. The bark is riddled with hundreds of bulging, popcorn-size hits. Made of sawdust, pitch, and bug scat, these spots mark where last year's hatch of adult beetles chewed their way in to lay their eggs, which turn larval by the fall. Infused with natural antifreeze that withstands temperatures down to thirty below, *D. ponderosae* larvae hibernate till summer, when they pupate, abandon their brood tree, and take flight to attack fresh stands. The short of it is, this green tree's a goner. By next spring the needles will fade; by summer, they'll turn red. Not some feel-good autumn-in-Vermont red, either. More like the rocker-panel rust on a junkyard Dodge.

There's something about a red evergreen that says we're deeply screwed. Take a drive over Montana's 6,320-foot MacDonald Pass and you'll see these trees by the millions, spilling down the Continental Divide like leftover marinara. Some ecologists say there's little to worry about from *D. ponderosae*. They're quick to point out that these beetles are endemic—that they've been around as long as the forests themselves, that they cull older, weaker trees, and that these outbreaks come and go naturally over the centuries.

But this time, most scientists say, things have changed. Stressed by less rainfall and a warmer climate, our high-altitude lodgepole stands can't muster enough pitch to flush out the invaders in the numbers the bug now presents. Frigid temperatures used to control the beetle population, killing off the majority each winter, but the last time my hometown of Helena saw sustained temperatures of thirty below was 1996. As populations continue to multiply, as they continue to thrive at higher elevations and latitudes and develop tastes for new species (the whitebark pine is now functionally extinct in some places), human intervention has so far proved maddeningly ineffective.

In short, there's never been a better time to be a beetle. With the forests spread before them like a posh cruise-ship buffet, and no serious predation to worry about, the beetles are writing a whole new script, one in which they're no longer mindless, ravening insects but a particularly exuberant tribe of eco-nihilists. Or perhaps just another billion-fold population of insatiable consumers and, in that way, not so different from us.

Nobody knows how all this will play out. But if conditions persist, hard-hit places like Colorado stand to lose virtually all of their mature lodgepole pines. High-altitude trees help retain winter snowpack; if they go into decline, spring runoffs could radically change, affecting local water management. In places like Yellowstone, the whitebark pine's anticipated demise will eliminate grizzly bears' primary food source, the tree's cones. And what happens when these billion or so carbon-absorbing trees decay and become carbon producers? The temperature goes up another notch.

At this point, the situation is much like what happens when a third world country unexpectedly goes nuclear: there's widespread alarm followed by a rush to learn about a long-ignored, now ominous population. Who are these bugs anyway, and what do they have in mind for the Rockies?

It's only natural that a panorama of several million dead pines would have a disquieting effect on the psyche.

Many think that should these red trees ignite, it will mean a cataclysmic fire of untold ferocity, one hot enough to vitrify the earth, scald the very air, and turn the verdant northern Rockies into a Mars-scape.

But some ecologists believe that red, dead trees are only moderately more flammable than live green ones and that—without the green trees' more volatile resins—they might actually burn cooler. That doesn't mean that fire danger is lower, says University of Colorado geography professor Tania Schoennagel. "Despite having recently come out of a fifteen-year drought," she points out, "Colorado can soon expect another. With or without the pine beetle, the potential for catastrophic fire is always there."

It seems like a stretch but, according to a recent Colorado State Forest Service release, we run a far greater risk of being hit by a tree while hiking than burning up in a fiery cataclysm. "[Beetle-killed trees] begin to fall within three to five years," the report explains. There are 550 miles of power lines and 954 miles of trails running through infested stands, and that's just in Colorado alone.

For both these reasons—fire and public safety—there's now an urgency to fell these hazard trees, as well as to create an unbroken line of fire-resistant redoubts in what the U.S. Forest Service likes to call "the Wildland Urban Interface"—the place where the buildings leave off and the woods begin.

In Helena this has created a boom of sorts for bonded contractors and the somewhat chancier element of out-of-work loggers and gypsy woodsmen. As it happens, I fall somewhere between these two tribes. I was a teacher until the economy went under, but for thirty years before that, I worked as an arborist. So last June, I dusted off my hard hat with my fellow recession-strafed friend Tom Harpole—himself a former coastal timber faller turned magazine writer—and contracted to clean up the woods around our pediatrician friends Mike and Tess's ski cabin, in the Flint Creek Range, ninety miles southwest of Helena.

On the drive over, Harp, an athletic, gently ravaged senior in a hickory shirt, tried out the results of his cataract surgery, reading me an article from the *Helena Independent Record*. Taken from Governor Brian Schweitzer's spring fire briefing, the piece basically informed readers that if they were dumb enough to build in the woods, they were pretty much on their own. "You have a personal responsibility," Schweitzer said. "Don't look to the government to bail you out."

Harp put down the paper and grinned. "Is that tough love or what?"

The idea behind a beetle "treatment," as the Forest Service calls it, is to ambush the bugs before they hatch out, which in Montana generally happens in late July. Harp and I would fell the brood trees—the ones with active larvae—and then cover the downed wood with black plastic, frying the hatch before the beetles could fly out to attack nearby trees.

We gassed up our saws and went to work. The affected three acres had upwards of 500 trees—two-thirds of them lodgepole, half of which were infested. Since it was a family cabin and small children were usually afoot, we felled other hazard trees, too: leaners (uprooted trees held up by their neighbors), widow-makers (detached tops hanging in the canopy), snags (rotten, unstable trees), and jackpots (an idiot's delight of leaners, snags, and widow-makers). I even climbed and topped two stricken lodgepoles that were uncomfortably close to the power lines.

It's been years since I spent a whole day felling trees, but the work felt much like it used to, which is to say hard, dirty, and dangerous. The only thing that had changed was the way such straightforward labor was now bedeviled by vagaries: Because of the magnitude of this outbreak, did it really matter if we covered our downed wood when the neighbors left their brood trees standing? Who were we kidding with this bit of woodland housekeeping?

Harp and I felled a lot of beetle kill that summer, specializing in higher-risk trees—the pines so close to buildings, propane tanks, and chicken coops that the other renegade sawyers wouldn't touch them. In August we bid on a job to remove three beetle-killed pines from the property of Harp's friend Perry, five miles west of Helena. The dead trees threatened the power lines, but Perry was most concerned for the six "focal" ponderosas by his house. These had a scattering of beetle hits at the base, so he wondered if we should just take them, too.

I told Perry with utmost confidence that, no, such a light scatter of hits meant that the pines had pitched the bugs out. I went on to announce that by this point the beetles had certainly hatched, but to be on the safe side he could spray them with the insecticide Carbaryl, arguably the most effective beetle deterrent on the market. Perry, a plumber by trade, wasted no time. The next day he rented a pressure sprayer and hosed down every viable pine he had.

When Harp and I returned five days later, we found a hatch in full progress. The insects had swarmed the house pines—the ones I'd presumed to call safe—and chewed through the Carbaryl like butterscotch. In spite of the rainy summer, the big pines offered little resistance. From the base up past the fifty-foot mark, thousands of entry holes peppered the trunks. There was nothing to do but remove them.

As I spiked my way up the first tree, I heard a commotion below. I planted my gaffs, hung back on my flip line, and peered down. Like a genie out of a bottle, a fresh hatch was boiling from the tree Harp had felled. They crawled up his Husqvarna, flew into his face, and in a moment fairly engulfed him. Frantically, Perry scraped clumps of them off Harp's shirt.

"Those fuckers were trying to take me down," Harp would tell me later.

"They mistook you for a pine," I said. "It could happen to anyone."

"No," he insisted. "This was personal. They infested me, Fred. I felt violated."

It was good for a laugh, but the incident continued to haunt me. The beetles had emerged weeks past the hatch window, attacked well-hydrated trees, and made a point of attacking not just mature trees but the saplings that would take their place. And they ate through fresh Carbaryl to do it. In the span of an afternoon, everything I thought I knew about this bug had been proven wrong.

At the Blackfoot Tap Room later that fall, I stood next to a strapping fireman named Scott Bockman who sprays Carbaryl on the weekends for extra cash. I mentioned the events out on Perry's spread: the swarming of Harp, the jailbreak hatch, the strange timing of it all. Scott laughed and bought me a beer.

"You can toss that 'hatch window' crap out with the term 'unseasonably warm,'" he said. "Near as I can tell, they hatch whenever they feel like it. As far as that goes, I've seen them attack spruce and Doug fir. Things are changing so fast out there, the science can't keep up."

For now, our efforts at beetle intervention have indeed seemed feeble. Carbaryl works in places, but nobody wants to talk about the collateral effects of a forest-wide application on honeybees and songbirds. Controlled burns sound neat, but a fire of that scale would be hard to control, and the bugs would already have left the red trees for live ones. So we make inroads where we can and cling to small victories when we find them.

Retired Colorado entomologist David Leatherman, who has studied these beetles for more than thirty years, offers a glimmer of hope. The past couple of years have brought anomalous weather patterns, he says, particularly to Colorado. Higher and faster summer winds have borne beetle hatches aloft, sometimes carrying them 150 miles or more—in one case as far as Nebraska. This might sound like yet another example of the climate accommodating the bug, helping them colonize, but such events can disperse the hatch, making it difficult for beetles to infest a pine with numbers large enough to kill it. Of 700 pines attacked in Fort Collins in 2008, Leatherman says, there was only a 10 percent mortality rate.

Meanwhile, scientists are finding ways to interrupt the beetles' highly successful cycle. The focus falls squarely on their sex life, something Leatherman makes sound downright erotic. "For openers," he says, "these guys have very short lives, and they spend 360 days of it in pitch dark. Then they pupate and suddenly they've got wings! They crawl out from under the bark, down a long tunnel, fly into a brilliant summer sky. Can you imagine? They float there in the dazzle, rise on the breeze, soar off on the scrumptious pheromone trails that the females—who hatched first—thoughtfully left behind."

The male follows this trail to the nuptial chamber that the female has prepared in the new brood tree, where he delivers a sequence of clicks, chirps, and squeaks that, according to Leatherman, comprises the standard pitch of every male looking to score:

"What's up? Nice place! I'll be gentle…"

A few years back, science broke in on this love fest with a synthetic pheromone called trans-verbenol, which mimics the hormonal "no vacancy" signal that *D. ponderosae* sends out when a pine is already full. Some ski areas—Sun Valley, for one—have broadcast verbenol by the planeload over its runs, while Aspen is painting it on individual trees.

And we're learning more about the bugs' love song itself. I recently purchased a CD of the pine beetles' vocal stylings. The audio was captured by New Mexico composer David Dunn, who poked a makeshift microphone into the phloem layer of a piñon pine infested with *Ips confusus* beetles, the *D. ponderosae* cousins that decimated southwestern piñon forests in the early 2000s. It's not Barry White, but there's an edginess to it, a rising bolero of cheeps, chirps, and scratchings. The ensemble features a rhythmic crunching sound, like an 1890's stamp mill, and a periodic flushing noise, like a line of public urinals, followed by a deep and melodious squeaking like a dry cork twisting in a bottle. It may never go platinum, but it's got an inter-phylum charm that could easily cross over.

Last winter, 2010, Northern Arizona University researchers Richard Hofstetter and Reagan McGuire employed a similar choir in their experiments with sonic-bullet-style beetle control. They'd already hit a *D. ponderosae* colony with high-volume Rush Limbaugh broadcasts, to no effect. They'd tried hip-hop. Again, nothing. But when they blasted a recording of re-mixed *D. ponderosae* "voices" at the colony, the beetles went insane. "There'd be a male and a female, they would mate... and two hours later, he'd chew her to pieces," said McGuire. "That's not natural."

Dunn, who consulted on the project, had mixed feelings about the results. "I fell in love with [these beetles]," he said. "But then, we're watching them cannibalize each other. I always think, 'How bad is this karma?'"

My own beetle karma caught up with me over Thanksgiving when I ran into Tess for the first time since that summer. I asked how her pines had fared and she gave me a rueful smile. "The beetles destroyed most everything," she said. "We need you to come back, I guess."

With millions of acres going red, I don't know why it was so hard to swallow. Of course, our efforts had come to nothing. Her woods were simply part of a rapidly changing landscape, and it was time I came to appreciate the scale of it.

Prankster, Pass By

In August 1964, I was idling away the afternoon at a Quaker country day school in Alexandria, Virginia, where I had a job lifeguarding for a summer camp program. It was a particularly tiny pool. I was twenty years old. I'd flunked out of two pretty good colleges and didn't have a clue about what was next. For this reason, I'd decided to become an author, consoling myself with the notion that my pratfalls and tomfoolery were but a means to gain the "real world" experience a writer needed. That afternoon, the pretty tennis coach with whom I'd shared my aspirations padded barefoot across the deck to hand me a copy of her favorite book, *One Flew Over the Cuckoo's Nest*.

By that time of day, the kids had all gone home and there was no one poolside but a pair of leathery old Quakers, quietly discussing the Mississippi Freedom Rides. Just nine months past JFK's assassination, it's fair to describe America as a bewildered and paranoid place, one keenly suspicious of the exotic, and getting more so all the time. I kicked back in my deck chair and began one of the most influential books I've ever read. There was no Siddhartha, no Holden Caulfield, no epic soldiery. Unlike the Shaw, Jones, or Mailer I'd read, the battle unfolded in a microcosm—between a fanatically repressive psychiatric nurse and an ungrammatical working tough of Promethean daring. Beyond this, the writing had a depth and richness that stemmed from a rarity at that time: an educated writer so comfortable with his blue collar roots, he effortlessly called up poetry from them. I decided there was nothing I wanted more in life than to possess this same ability, and for the ensuing forty years, Ken Kesey remained an influence I couldn't shake; part inspiration, part spirit guide, and part cautionary tale. After his early novels drew comparisons to Tolstoy, Kesey would put his writing on hold to become a career ecstatic.

My hunger for "real world" experience didn't preclude a lateral career move or two; a year later, I found my-self living in Boston, a twenty-one-year-old husband and father to be, working days and going to school nights. With its quotidian routine of fatherhood and academia, my life seemed less Kesey-like than even my kiddy-pool gig the year before. Since I hadn't thought to separate him from his characters, it was some time before I learned that Kesey, like me, had been a scholar and father, too. A guy who, to make ends meet, did what any family man would do: he hired himself out as pharmaceutical guinea pig.

In Autumn of 1965 the term "cultural upheaval" didn't exist yet, but even if you managed to tune out the murders in Mississippi and the mounting Viet Nam disquiet, you really couldn't miss the urban riots. A psychic tem-blor traveled the mantle of this country; a troubled, antsy feeling of a force gathering strength and mass.

I'd been too busy to think much about Kesey until I read in *Esquire* he'd left writing to become Master of Revels for the Merry Pranksters, a kind of ecstatics-with-out-borders performance group. With much of their act a complete hallucination, the Pranksters were unlike any-thing America had seen, traveling the country in a school bus called *Further*, just to goof on what they saw. To be part of this Zeitgeist Express, to be "on the bus" with Kesey, I thought, I would gladly give up everything I had.

Meanwhile, my friends and I made do with our own LSD experiments, but without the West Coast production values. We found that, except for the fact it lasted twelve hours and you never knew where it might take you or leave you off, it was a pretty good time. But it scared my wife badly. In fact it scared me more than I liked to admit, which, I imagined could only hurt my Prankster prospects.

Like every marriage I knew of, my own failed to nego-tiate the sixties. After the divorce, I abandoned graduate studies, found myself unceremoniously without family, career, or clue. By 1969, the landscape was looking bleak. Kesey was in jail, and after the Tet offensive and the King and Kennedy shootings, most people were glad to see that the flower-power deal was over.

For a grad school dropout and part time lifeguard, the job market wasn't all it could be. I moved from our Back Bay apartment to a cheap Cambridge studio across the river. It reeked of scorched rice and hashish oil. A band called "The Glass Bead Game" cohabitated overhead, and in the course of an increasingly futile job search, I picked up *Sometimes a Great Notion* and read it in a twenty-hour sitting. Besides the fact it featured a grad-school type even more clueless than me, there was a terrific scene with Leland's half-brother Hank, high in a Douglas fir top, rigging it for a tail-spar. When I finally put the book down I thought: If only I had a job as a Cambridge high-lead logger, I'd never take any shit again!

In yet another lateral career move, I found work at the necktie and cravat counter in the MIT Coop men's department, where, at the very height of the counter culture, I was actually *required* to wear a jacket and tie. I recall thinking, if the characters in *Great Notion* were forged in a crucible of the Pacific Northwoods, the kind of character forged in the Coop Men's Wear section was probably better not to know.

In February 1969 a furious Northeaster blew in off the Atlantic, pummeled the coastal forest, broke the great shade trees of Boston into matchwood. The next morning I woke to the high and predatory wail of a chainsaw under full throttle. Badly hung over, I peered east into the spring sunlight to see a bare-headed guy in a canvas jacket climb sixty feet up the big sycamore next door. I could see the cloud of his breath as he belayed himself off the shattered top, then swung around to the overhanging front of the stem so that his belly was to its curvature. He tested his rigging, planted his feet. Snow pockets sparkled in the crotches above him as he raised his saw and cut a bold, deep notch, inches in front of his face! It appeared he would shortly cut himself out of the tree, but he swung niftily back to the other side, re-belayed to make the back cut, and sent five-hundred pounds of broken sycamore to the pavement. He paused there to smoke a cigarette while I tried to make sense of what I'd seen. It was bolder than even Hank Stamper. A man who could do *that*, I imagined, could do *anything*.

When I finally caught up with him, Kesey was shorter than I'd imagined, soft-spoken, almost wistful—in that way people get when they take a bath in LSD. It was 1978, and I was a tree climber in Boulder Colorado. There was a rumor he'd finished a *Great Notion* sequel, and so it was standing room only at the Naropa Kerouac School of Disembodied Poetics where he was due to give a reading. In honor of the occasion, I chose to wear my climbing duds; Westco boots and a pair of Lee "88" logger's jeans, in the belief that from my outfit, any fool could see I was the real deal, not another hyper-educated Boulder pseud.

He didn't read from a *Great Notion* sequel, he read a non-fiction piece set on his family farm near Eugene. It began as a story about basic animal husbandry, in particular, a fated Aberdeen seed bull named "Abdul." Then, like all good stories, it spun off into something ever larger. There was nary a mention of a caulk-booted logger, so that I gradually felt uncomfortable in my woodsman's drag, like I'd showed up at Easter all dressed for Halloween.

I thought to approach him afterwards, but there was a thicket of admirers surrounding him and I had a paralyzing attack of shyness. Really, what did I have to say but that his books made me badly want to resemble his fictional characters? By this logic, I should now turn in my Lee "88s" for bib overalls and manure boots. I'd entertained the bonehead fallacy you became the character to earn the story, and up to this moment I'd not been able to see it. I retreated to the men's room, so distracted by my revelation that I mistook a stock-tank looking wash trough for a urinal. I'd just unbuttoned my "88" jeans when a gruff old gent strolled in, took one look, and blanched. "Hey!" he finally sputtered. "You can't piss *here*!"

While I spent the 1970s climbing for every piratical dingdong who ever made a buck off a tree, my University of Montana MFA classmates were fresh-faced and unsullied. They were better read, had actually written stories, and most of them cared little about the life of hard-knocks I'd bet the farm on. A few older writers, however, did. Now in our thirties, we vetted each other's authenticity, embraced the style known as "dirty realism," and wrote stories about hard-living tradesmen, Nam vets and guys who didn't take any shit. We thought it dishonest to write of things purely imagined rather than things we'd actually done. Possibly this came from a suspicion contemporary fiction was dominated by bloodless East Coast aesthetes whose privileged lives made them contemptuous of the world as we knew it. Or possibly it was just a hedge against the limits of our talent.

Throughout it all, I maintained the belief that my connection to Kesey was unique. Had he not, after all, transformed me from a lowly cravat salesman to a genuine hard-nosed high-limb man? I was surprised to discover how many of my writer friends felt a similar connection, and it took me a while to understand that this was one of Kesey's gifts.

But as the 1970s rolled into the next decade, we weren't hearing much from Ken Kesey. We worried over his lack of output, but since it was a fact he was also a tireless explorer of inner space, we were ready to cut him that slack. There could be no way of measuring this, but he and his friends likely got higher than any human beings ever had, maybe oozed through the membrane between this world and the ineffable. Some of us speculated Kesey might have *outgrown* writing. I mean, after you've been "Further," where do you go from there?

Extremophilia

Eventually my fiction professor, Bill Kittredge, mentioned the Wallace Stegner fellowship at Stanford. The lucky recipient got a free year of writing time with stipend and a move to San Francisco thrown in. Kesey and many of my favorite writers had been there, so I applied on a lark and forgot about it, was, in fact actively pursuing my real-life business with trees when Stanford called with the news. My God, I thought, this changes *everything*!

I'd followed Kesey into the trees, followed him west, followed him into writing. Now I was lucky enough to follow him to Stanford. It pleased me to think that he more than most would appreciate our arrival in a rack-bed Chevy dump truck.

With its palm-lined drive and red tile roofs, bicycling from Palo Alto to the eight-thousand-acre Stanford campus felt like going to work at a movie set. Back then, Creative Writing was in Building 50, the big sandstone building next to the chapel. At the round table in the Jones Library, a forty-year succession of emerging writers engaged in everything from point-of-view discussion to the exquisite kind of character assassination endemic to workshops everywhere.

While I hadn't imagined Stanford still pickled in acid, when I mentioned Kesey to veterans of those times, a wariness flickered briefly. I got a sense that if the topic wasn't quite taboo, it fell into the Been There, Done That category, and there was a suggestion that Stanford was a more serious place, past the well-documented excesses of the 1960s. Or the even the low-rent bacchanalias of the 1970s where, for example, Ray Carver might devour a whole birthday cake, or non-lactating women try their hand at nursing an infant. Or more to the point, where you never knew who you might wake up with.

The closest I came to the wild heart of those times was an ill-conceived celebration of my appointment as Jones lecturer. Festivities began at our apartment on Tasso Street, then were to move on to a larger venue on Waverly, where the whole Creative Writing department would be in attendance. My party was a modest one; a few friends, a case of beer, a quart of Bushmills and a cache of psilocybin mushrooms someone thoughtfully left open like a bag of Doritos. Eventually, I came to assume the whole gang had eaten them, and that they couldn't be very strong, because nobody was acting particularly weird. In both cases, I was wrong. They were *very* strong, and the only other guy eating them was the lone party crasher. I watched him while he seemed to turn bright red. I liked that about him, since I was turning bright red, too. We found this fact hilarious. Then everything was hilarious, so there was no real point in trying to stop laughing. We kept on goofing till my new friend finally wandered downstairs and off into the neighborhood, issuing regular peals of laughter, like a fruit bat sounding the night.

At this point I made the mistake of looking in a mirror. Not only was I bright red, there was something very wrong with my face. I began to get a feeling that, next party on, the laughs might get scarce. The department chair would be there, and maybe Wallace Stegner himself, who was known to frown on such hi-jinks. I'd need my fellow fruit-bat if I was going to pull this off, but he was half-way to Vacaville by then. I was in a jam. I was a *lecturer,* junior faculty, and in it for the long haul. In fact, I was now a company man, and arriving in the guise of a rubber-lipped maniac could in some way damage my creditability. At least, this is what I told myself.

I walked to the party, battened down the hatches well

as I could, but still managed to cause problems. To relieve pressure in my brain, I yawned and gulped continuously, like an airplane passenger at altitude. It eventually freaked out the hot tub crowd, who asked me politely to leave. Since I had no idea what might come out of my mouth, I dummied up completely, became so grave in aspect that a friend afterwards said, "Wow, what *happened* to you last night, man? You looked like you were playing chess with Death."

Of *course* the Pranksters were long gone. The 1988 Bush landslide was enough to rain on any parade. The Loma Prieta earthquake broke up Stanford's fabled archways while the orchard lands to the north were ground zero for the coming information juggernaut. The kids going to Dead concerts were so young, they looked more like anime happenings than anything to do with the Sixties. It was a time when aging writers thought hard about career; how fierce was the competition for jobs, how the days when you got by on charm and who you got high with were drying up. Oddly, there was another psychopharmaceutical revolution, but instead of the tried and true "systematic derangement of the senses," people were taking Prozac.

My wife Caroline reminded me of a dinner in Cupertino with a couple of Knight-Ridder fellows we'd befriended. We'd brought a good bottle of wine to share and were surprised to find, in a company of journalists, there were no takers at all. When we asked them why, they confided that, since they were now completely "at ease" with themselves, they no longer felt the need to "self-medicate."

Our last year in Palo Alto, I started to read *Sailor's Song*, but it seemed painfully dated, so I set it down and put things in perspective. At the very least, Kesey wrote two terrific novels, both of which are still in print today. He was a great champion of the more altered states and, depending on who you talked to, he either invented a whole new culture or, like Charlie Parker ten years earlier, turned many young artists onto serious dope such that they soon left their best work behind them. At the same time, he set me and others on the road to writer-hood, though it was never very clear how all that worked. So what the hell else did I want from the guy—to gain his blessing, too?

I'd heard Kesey had been ill, so I was not surprised to read of his passing. What's more, fall of 2001, with the millennium spectacularly unpromising, it seemed a better time than most to leave this earth. But for the first time in a while, I regretted I never met him. I guess I always wanted to tell him my story. As soon as I made it good enough. But mostly it made me recall a peculiar event near the end of my Stanford tenure.

My office was on the ground floor of Building 50, halfway between the East and West entrances. The main doors, seven feet tall and sheathed in brass, stayed locked throughout the weekends. On a beautiful Saturday, spring of 1991, I was squirreled away there, working on my novel. I'd spent a lot of time on it, hoped to sell it before I left, and in this way make the kind of triple somersault style career move that would insure I never climbed another tree again. I was holed up, working my eyes red, when there came a sudden knocking on the west door.

At this point, a quick word about this novel. Not surprisingly, it was a book about guys who work in the trees.

But while it started out as a sprawling long form, I felt increasingly the need to cut it, that my material, after all, was not that interesting. The more I mistrusted it, the more I tried to soften the books grittier aspects with an increasingly distilled language. I spent hundreds of hours, cutting and buffing, till the book was barely novella-sized. And through it all, I'd placed a secret reference—my ace in the hole, you could say—which I'd cunningly spun through like a thread of silver. Without going into detail, it was a reference so obscure, so perfectly hermetic, that unless you happened to be a scholar of early Celtic nature poetry, you might wonder why someone would write such a book.

Meanwhile, the racket at the west door had gone from a knocking to a pounding to a full out fusillade of thumping you'd associate with a raiding party or ATF flying squad. At this point I figured, whoever would make a racket like that was not someone I wanted to deal with. Once again, I battened the hatches down, kept plugging away.

In the next morning's paper was an oddly familiar picture of a 1939 IH school bus. Painted every color known to man, its destination window said "Further." It was the bus; the one you were either on or off! And next to it was Kesey, Babbs, and the gang, in town for a Prankster retrospective! The racket in Building 50 had to be them. The Sixties came back for me in a turbo blast from the past! And I blew it! But how could I know this for sure? I stewed over it a long while before deciding it was best not to know. Otherwise, I was Gabriel Conroy in Joyce's story "The Dead," mistaking Gretta's reverie for a booty call.

Eventually, my novel became so rarified it actually vanished into thin air. Bought by a small Texas press, it went all the way to galleys only to be tossed, mysteriously, to the void. It's hard to know what happened, but I suspect that someone finally read it. Meanwhile, discouraged with my attempts at a suitably transcendent prose, I turned to non-fiction, for which I seemed to have more knack. Sometimes I wondered, was that actually the Pranksters, tripping down the Santa Cruz mountains just to bang on the Building 50 door? And what are you supposed to do when the Sixties come calling for you? Drop a tab of Purple Haze and slather yourself with patchouli?

I understand now that despite the long, demi-association, I was never meant to party with the Pranksters, and that I'd followed Kesey for as far as I'd been able. I needed to finally make it or break it, the last thing I needed was a flying circus. Like the guy in the tree I once saw, there was a time I thought he could do anything, but this proved not necessarily to be the case. Mostly it was all a measure of how badly I needed to believe such things.

A month after Kesey's passing, I e-mailed Ken Babbs and recalled the dates for him.

"Yeah," he replied. "Yeah, we were around campus about then. You know, come to think about it, that might have been us."

"So what were you guys doing, banging the door like you lost your minds?"

"How the hell would I know? That was all so long ago."

Acknowledgments

The author would like to thank the Ucross Foundation and the Fine Arts Work Center for the invaluable space and time.

CPSIA information can be obtained at www.ICGtesting.com
Printed in the USA
BVOW042134101111

275832BV00001B/10/P

9 780982 860137